Best of Humour

Compiled by Rewa Mirpuri

PUBLISHED BY THE
INTERNATIONAL SERVICE COMMITTEE OF
ROTARY CLUB OF SINGAPORE
TEL: (65) 6737 2504, FAX: (65) 6732 8535

ISBN NO. 981-04-8555-7

© **Copyright Rewa Mirpuri, 2004**

All rights reserved. No part of this publication may be produced, stored in a retrieval system, or transmitted in any form or by any means, electronic, mechanical, photocopying, recording, or otherwise, without the prior permission of the compiler.

**Published by The Rotary Club of Singapore
Tel: (65) 6737 2504, Fax: (65) 6732 8535**

Editor: Penny Reutens
Cover Design: Carl Ferrao

Printed in Singapore

First Published in June 2004

First Reprint — February 2005

ROTARY CLUB OF SINGAPORE
DISTRICT 3310

FOREWORD

This is a success story par excellence. Thanks to Rotarian Rewa Mirpuri's simple idea to help raise funds for a good cause, the "BOOK OF HUMOUR" reached fantastic levels of success:-

80,000 copies sold and in its 21st reprint

The new **"BEST OF HUMOUR"** book is a totally new edition, which everyone should own and read. I have no doubt that it will be a runaway success again.

In addition, the money raised will go towards the less fortunate globally, through the Rotary movement worldwide.

What a wonderful way to "CELEBRATE ROTARY"
for its 100th Year of caring for the Community.

Dr Ivor Thevathasan JP
CENTENARY GOVERNOR
ROTARY INTERNATIONAL
DISTRICT 3310

ROTARY CLUB OF SINGAPORE
DISTRICT 3310

MESSAGE

The publication of the **Best of Humour** aptly coincides with the celebration of the 75th anniversary of the Club. It is a dedication to community service to augment the success of the first Book of Humour and to provide needful resource for World Community Service.

The tireless effort of Rewa Mirpuri, friends and fellow-Rotarians in compiling material of a subject with an ageless nature should find appeal with Rotarians and people of all ages alike. Your support will help to bring aid and relief through Rotary assistance to the needy.

Tan Chin Ngiap
President, 2004-2005
Rotary Club of Singapore

PREFACE

Thank you, thank you, thank you very much for your great support of my first book, **Book of Humour**, now in its 21ST Reprint with over 80,000 copies sold.

The astounding success of this first book rekindled my excitement in this project and further motivated me to come out with this new second edition, **BEST OF HUMOUR**.

With the help of many friends and well wishers, I have collated a new, choice collection of the funniest, side-splitting jokes for your enjoyment. I am sure you will relish these funnies as much as I have in compiling them.

Once again the proceeds of this book will go towards helping the poor and the needy in the disaster stricken countries around the world, under the flag of The Rotary Club of Singapore.

So lets enjoy the book, laugh and bring "sunshine" to the less fortunate.

HAPPY READING.

....
Rewa Mirpuri

ACKNOWLEDGEMENT

This book is dedicated to all those who helped towards its creation.

The book would not have been possible without the kind help, support and contributions from all friends, well wishers, members of the Rotary Club of Singapore and the family of compiler, Rewa Mirpuri.

It would be difficult to pinpoint names as so many have helped in one way or another - like in evaluation and contribution of jokes, editing, cover design ideas, etc. It would not be fair to all concerned, to mention only a few names.

Knowing that this book is being produced for a good cause, everyone generously gave a helping hand and made this edition, for which special appreciation is acknowledged.

Contents

The dating game	1
Marriage…for better or for worse	5
Husbands and wives	25
Men and Women	52
Men are… Women are	61
He says…She says	62
Parents and Kids	63
Mothers-In-Law	76
Maids – the paid help…	78
Faith – fully yours	80
At the Pearly Gates	95
At the bar	98
School – the best years of our life	100
Animals and Such	107
Airlines…	109
A taxing matter	112
Computer savvy	113
Lawyers and Judges	114
Are blondes really dumb…?	119
Country bumpkins	123
Politically correct	128
Golf – all in the game	131
Doctors and Patients	134
The Viagra syndrome	149
Telling signs	150
All the nations	153
Business	158
New Definitions	160

> **"A good laugh is sunshine in the house"**
>
> *William Makepeace Thackeray*

Please consume this book in the light-hearted spirit it was compiled, and not as "FACTS OF LIFE". These jokes were compiled to evoke laughter - for a good cause. Censoring jokes that might have offended doctors, husbands, wives and mothers-in-law, etc. would have resulted in no book at all! Thank you!

The dating game

Divine Providence ...

A girl brings her fiancé home for dinner. After dinner, the fiancé and the girl's father go into the study for a man-to-man talk.
"So, what are you doing right now?" asks the father.
"I'm a theology scholar," replies the fiancé.
"Do you have any plans for employment?"
"I will study and God will provide."
"What about the children?" asks the father.
"God will provide."
"And your house and car?"
"Again, God will provide," says the fiancé.
After the talk, the girl's mother asks the father, "So what did both of you talk about?"
The father replies, **"He has no plans of employment, but on the other hand, he thinks I'm God!!"**

All he wants ...

Two friends, Dave and John are talking about their love life.
Dave: "So, John, how's it going with the ladies?"
John: "All women are nothing but sex objects."
Dave: "Really?"
John: "Yep. Whenever I mention sex, they object!!"

Return to sender ...
A soldier serving overseas is reading a letter from his sweetheart. To his surprise, she has written to tell him that she is breaking off their engagement and that she wants him to return her photograph.
So, he goes out and collects from his friends all the unwanted photographs of women that he can get, bundles them together and sends them to her with a note saying: **"I regret I cannot remember which picture is yours -- please keep your photo and return the others!"**

The perfect match
A young lady, desperately in need of a love match, arranges an appointment with a professional matchmaker: "I'm looking for a spouse. Can you please help me find a suitable one?"
Matchmaker: "Your requirements please."
Young lady: "Well, let me see, he needs to be good-looking, polite, humorous, sporty, knowledgeable, good at singing and dancing; willing to keep me company the whole day at home during my leisure hours, if I don't go out; able to tell me interesting stories when I need a companion for conversation and be silent when I want to rest."
The matchmaker listened thoughtfully and replied,
"I understand. You need a television!"

Show off
To impress his date, the young man took her to a very chic Italian restaurant. After sipping some fine wine, he picked up the menu and ordered.
"We'll have the Giuseppe Spomdalucci," he said.
"Sorry, sir," said the waiter. "**That's the owner!!**"

Bind date woes
College student: "How was your blind date?"
Roommate: "Terrible! He showed up in his 1932 Rolls Royce."
College student: "Wow! That's a very expensive car. What's so bad about that?"
Roommate: "He was the original owner!!"

Fatal attraction
Desperate boyfriend: "Sir, your daughter says she loves me, and she can't live without me, and she wants to marry me."
Parent: "And you're asking my permission to marry her?"
Desperate boyfriend: **"No, I'm asking you to make her leave me alone!"**

Women don't make fools of men – most of them are the do-it-yourself types!

Spank me honey ...
A young guy was complaining to his Boss about the problems he was having with his stubborn girlfriend.

"She gets me so angry sometimes, I could hit her," the young man exclaimed.

"Well, I'll tell you what I used to do with my wife," the Boss replied. "Whenever she got out of hand I'd take her pants down and spank her."

Shaking his head the young guy replied, **"That doesn't work. Once I get her pants off, I'm not mad anymore!"**

Happiness
To be happy with a man, you must understand him a lot and love him a little.

To be happy with a woman, you must love her a lot and not try to understand her at all!

Propensity to change
A woman marries a man expecting him to change, but he doesn't.

A man marries a woman expecting that she won't change, and she does!

Success is a relative term. It brings so many relatives.

❖

Marriage...for better or for worse

Every husband needs a counsellor...
After just a few years of marriage, filled with constant arguments, a young man and his wife decided to consult a marriage counsellor to save their marriage.
Counsellor: "What seems to be the problem?"
Before the husband could say a word, the wife began talking 90 miles an hour about the short comings in their married life. After 15 minutes of listening to the wife, the counsellor went over to her, picked her up by her shoulders, kissed her passionately for several minutes, and then sat her down. The wife sat there speechless.
The counsellor then looked at the husband who was staring in disbelief at what had happened and said:
"Your wife NEEDS that at least twice a week!"
The husband scratched his head and replied, **"I can bring her here every Tuesday and Thursday!!"**

❖

A package deal!
Complete set of Encyclopaedia Britannica.
45 volumes. Excellent condition. $1,000.00 or best offer. No longer needed. Got married last weekend. Wife knows everything.

Paradise Lost ...
A woman woke in the middle of the night to the sound of desperate sobbing downstairs.
She looked all around and found her husband crouched in the corner, facing the wall, and sobbing.
"What's wrong with you?" she asked him.
"Remember when you were 16 and your father caught us having sex?" he replied.
"And remember, he gave me two choices - either marry you, or spend the next 20 years in prison."
Baffled, she said, "Yes, I remember, so what?"
"I would have been released today!!"

Paradise Regained ...
A Funeral service is being held in a synagogue for a woman who just passed away.
At the end of the service the pallbearers are carrying the casket out, when they accidentally bump into a wall, jarring the casket. They hear a faint moan.
They open the casket and find that the woman is alive. In fact, she lives for ten more years!!!
Alas, she finally dies and the funeral is again held at the same synagogue. At the end of the ceremony, the pallbearers are carrying out the casket. As they are walking down the aisle, the husband cries out …
"**Watch out for the wall!!!**"

Doris was fleeing from a fire in her home. She carried a dog in her lap.

Fireman: Lady is your husband still in the house.

"Yes," replied the woman.

"Then why don't you get him out instead of the dog? He'll burn to death."

"Don't worry," replied the woman **"He wont burn, he's taking a shower."**

The doctor and his wife were having a heated argument at breakfast.

As he stormed out of the house, the man angrily yelled to his wife, "You aren't that good in bed either!"

By midmorning, he decided he'd better make amends and phoned home.

After many rings, his wife, clearly out of breath, answered the phone.

"What took you so long to answer and why are you panting?"

"I was in bed."

"What in the world are you doing in bed at this hour?"

"Getting a second opinion!!"

You have two choices in life: you can stay single and be miserable; or get married and wish you were dead.

Some skills can be learnt ...
Marco: "Wow! This is a great meal! I knew my boss had a beautiful wife, but I didn't know you were a fantastic cook as well."
Boss' wife: "I think I should warn you, Marco, that I expect my husband home in an hour."
Marco: "But I'm not doing anything."
Boss' wife: "I know. I just wanted to let you know how much time you had!"

Smith goes to see his supervisor in the front office. "Boss," he says, "we're doing some heavy housecleaning at home tomorrow, and my wife needs me to help with the attic and the garage, moving and hauling stuff."
"We're short-handed, Smith" the boss replies. "I can't give you the day off."
"Thanks, boss," says Smith **"I knew I could count on you!"**

Longevity
Married men live longer than single men, but married men are more willing to die.

A man owes his success to his first wife and his second wife to his success.

The 'headache' ...
A husband, his wife and a group went on a hunting expedition. The pair got lost from the group.
A Gorilla jumped on the wife and started tearing her clothes off.
The wife shouted, "Darling! Help! What shall I do?"
Husband: **"Don't worry. Tell him you've got a headache and turn your back to him, he'll go away!"**

...And the 'remedy'
"The thrill is gone from my marriage," Bill tells his friend Doug.
Doug suggests, "Why not add some intrigue to your life and have an affair?"
"But what if my wife finds out?" asks Bill.
"Heck, this is a new age we live in, Bill. Go ahead and tell her about it!" says Doug.
So Bill went home and said, "Dear, I think an affair will bring us closer together."
"Forget it," said his wife. **"I've tried that - it didn't work!!"**

Are condoms really safe?
Condoms aren't completely safe. A friend of mine was wearing one and got hit by a bus.

Some suggestions work ... and some don't
A married guy called up his best buddy and said, "I don't know what to get my wife for her birthday - she has everything, and besides, she can afford to buy anything she wants, so I'm stumped."

His friend said, "I have an idea - why don't you make up a certificate saying she can have 60 minutes of great sex, any way she wants it - she'll probably be thrilled."

The next day his friend called, "Well? Did you take my suggestion?"

"Yes, I did," said the guy.

"Did she like it?" his friend asked.

"Oh yes! She jumped up, thanked me, kissed me on the forehead and ran out the door, yelling, **"I'll be back in an hour!!"**

At a staff meeting the Boss felt that he wasn't getting any respect.

The next day he brought in a small sign that read, **'I'm the Boss'**. He then taped it to his office door.

Later that day when he returned from lunch, he found that someone had taped a note to the sign that said, **"Your wife called, she wants her sign back!"**

A good wife always forgives her husband when she knows she's wrong.   Milton Berle

Honesty is the best policy ...
A married man was having an affair with his secretary. One day, their passions overcame them. They went to her house and made passionate love all afternoon. Exhausted from the wild sex, they fell asleep, awakening around 8 pm.
After the man put on his clothes, he took his shoes outside and rubbed them through the grass and dirt.
Then he slipped into his shoes and drove home.
"Where have you been!" demanded his wife when he entered the house.
"Darling, I can't lie to you. I've been having an affair with my secretary and we've been having sex all afternoon. I fell asleep and didn't wake up until eight o'clock."
The wife glanced down at his shoes and said, **"You lying bastard! You've been playing golf again!!"**

An elderly couple, Georgia and Fred, sit down to their Thanksgiving dinner.
Before eating, his wife remarks, "Has our 50 years of marriage made you grateful?"
"Yes, indeed!" Fred replied. **"I am grateful for the twenty years I was a bachelor!"**

Love thy neighbour ...
When the husband arrived home from office, his wife said, "Darling, could you please change the bulbs in our living room lights?"
Husband: "Am I an electrician?"
The next day, she approached her husband again, "Dear, would you please fix the leaky bathroom tap?"
"Am I a plumber?" retorted the husband.
The following day, the husband arriving home from work finds everything fixed.
"Who fixed it?" he asked his wife.
"Our helpful next-door neighbour," replied the wife.
"Did he ask for anything," enquired the curious husband.
"Yes dear," he requested that I either bake a cake for him or sleep one night with him."
"So, you baked him a big cake?" asked the husband.
The wife replied, **"Am I a baker?!"**

This couple had no children. Their neighbour had seven children. The husband went to the neighbour for guidance. "This Saturday," suggested his neighbour, "take her out to her favourite restaurant, order a bottle of the best wine, and dine in candle light. After dinner bring her home and open a bottle of the best champagne. Take off all her clothes and make her lie down in bed."
"Then?" asked the husband.
"Then just call me!!" said the neighbour.

Who's the Boss...?
A young honeymoon couple were undressing for bed. The husband, a big burly man, tossed his trousers to his bride and said, "Here, put these on."
She put them on. "I can't wear your trousers," she said, "they're huge!"
"That's right," said the husband, "and don't you ever forget it. I wear the pants in this family."
At that, she flipped him her panties and said, "Try these on."
He tried, unsuccessfully and said, "Hell! I can't get into your panties!"
"That's right," she retorted, **"and that's the way it's going to stay until your attitude changes!"**

Psychiatrist: "You don't have to let your wife henpeck you anymore. Go home and show her **YOU** are the boss."
The newly assertive husband rushes home and growls at his wife, "From now on, I'm the one giving orders around here. I want my supper right now, and when you get it on the table, go upstairs, and lay out my best clothes. Tonight, I'm going out with the boys and you are going to stay at home where you belong. And another thing.... you know who's going to comb my hair, button my shirt, and then tie my tie?"
"I certainly do," says his wife calmly, **"the undertaker!!!"**

It's better to have loved and lost ...
A man went for an exciting drive in his brand new BMW convertible. He stepped on the accelerator sending the needle shooting to over 140 km/h.
Then, seeing flashing red and blue lights behind him, He slowed down and pulled over to the side of the highway.
After examining his license and car, the officer said,
"Listen, it's been a long day. This is the end of my shift and it's Friday. I don't feel like more paperwork. If you can give me an excuse for your speeding that I haven't heard before, you can go."
The guy thought for a second and said: "Last week my wife ran off with a cop. I was afraid you were trying to give her back."
"Have a nice weekend," said the officer.

His & Her Future ...
A woman worries about the future until she gets a husband.
A man never worries about the future until he gets a wife.

Marriages are made in heaven. But so again, are thunder and lightning.

On second thoughts ...
A woman is walking on the road when a voice shouts out, "Don't take a step further." She obeys and suddenly a ton of bricks falls on the place where she would have been.
She thinks she imagined it and keeps walking until suddenly the voice calls out again. "Don't take a step further." She stops and a car skids past.
Then suddenly she hears the voice saying "I am your guardian angel, and I will warn you before anything bad happens to you. Now do you have any questions to ask me?"
"Yes!" shouts the woman, **"Just where were you on my wedding day!"**

Comprehension
There are two times when a man doesn't understand a woman – before marriage and after marriage.

I was having a walk at the Botanical Gardens when I saw a couple having a walk, with the wife's arms around her husband's waist.
I said to them, "You look a happy married couple."
"Yes," replied the guy with a long face, **"I am married ..... She is happy."**

15

Who's sorry now?
A guy was kneeling down by the grave, crying his heart out. "Oh why did you have to die? Why did you have to die?"
A passer by, touched by the scene, placed an arm on his shoulders, "Come, come I know how you feel, was this your father? Or your mother?"
"No, No," cried the man again, "Oh why did you have to die... "
"Was this your wife?" asked the passer by again.
"No, No, Oh why did he have to die...."
"For God's sake, tell me who it is."
"He was my wife's first husband," groaned the guy.

Every man should marry. After all, happiness is not the only thing in life.

A guy, in his office, was boasting to his friend how much he loved his wife.
A friend asked him, "What is the colour of her eyes?"
The guy was speechless. He didn't know.
Immediately he went home and entered the bedroom. The wife was lying on the bed with her eyes open. He looked at her eyes and said, "Ah, brown."
Hearing this Mr Brown came out from under the bed and said, **"How the hell did you know I was here??"**

2 Rings ... Wedding-ring & Suffer-ring

An elderly woman decided to have her portrait painted. She told the artist, "Paint me with diamond ear rings, a diamond necklace, emerald bracelets, a ruby brooch and a gold Rolex."

The confused artist said, "But you're not wearing any of those things."

"I know," she said, "but, if I die before my husband, I'm sure my husband will remarry. **I want his new wife to go crazy looking for the jewellery!"**

A dietician was addressing a large audience in Chicago.

"The material we put into our stomach is the cause of our suffering. Red meat is awful. Soft drinks erode your stomach lining. Chinese food is loaded with MSG. But, there is one thing more dangerous than anything else. Can anyone here tell me what food causes the most grief and suffering for years after eating it?"

A 75-year-old man in the front row stood up, and mournfully, said, **"The Wedding cake!"**

Memory

Any married man should forget his mistakes; there's no use in two people remembering the same thing!

Sporting spouses
The instructor was teaching the group of pregnant women who had come along with their spouses on how to breathe properly and the benefit of walking.
"Ladies," he announced, "Walking is especially beneficial at this stage. And, gentlemen, please take time and go walking with your partner."
The room went silent. Finally a man in the middle of the group raised his hand.
"Yes?" asked the teacher.
"Is it all right if she carries a golf bag while we walk?"

A man was sitting at the Super Bowl in the very best seat available.
The guy on his left noticed there was an empty seat next to him and said, "Can you believe someone actually paid for that seat and didn't come to the game?"
The fellow next to him replied, "Actually that's my wife's seat...we bought these tickets months ago. Unfortunately, my wife passed away so I came alone."
"I'm sorry to hear that, but why didn't you give the ticket to a family member or friend?"
"Oh, they're all at the funeral!!"

True worth...
Tom's wife wasn't very attractive, but he was no oil painting, either.
After the ceremony, Tom asked the vicar how much it all cost.
"Just give me what you think it's worth to have this lady for your wife," replied the Reverend.
Tom looked at his wife, and handed the vicar $50.
The vicar looked at Tom's wife and **gave him $42 change!!**

Q: Why are married women heavier than single women?
A: Single women come home, see what's in the fridge and go to bed.
Married women come home, see what's in the bed and go to the fridge.

Before marriage, a man yearns for the woman he loves. After marriage, the 'Y' becomes silent.

My wife told me the car wasn't running well because there was water in the carburettor. I asked where the car was, she told me, **"In the lake."**

A husband said to his wife, "Jina, you have a lovely voice. You sing very well."
"How nice of you to say so!" replied Jina. "I wish I could say the same about your voice and singing."
"There is nothing to stop you. If I can tell a lie, so can you."

❖

Spare words ...
A man died and his wife phoned the newspaper to place an obituary. She called the obituary department and said, "This is what I want to print: **'Bernie is dead.'** "
The man at the newspaper said, "But for $25 you are allowed to print six words."
The woman answered, "OK. Then print:
'Bernie is dead. Toyota for sale.' "

❖

A husband noticed that his wife always carried a picture of his in her handbag and then go to work. Curious he asked her the reason.
"Well dear," she said, "every time I have any problems, no matter how difficult and insurmountable they are, I look at your picture and they all disappear."
Flattered, he said, "Well darling you see how powerful and miraculous I am for you?"
"Yes Dear," she replied, "when I look at your picture I say to myself, **'what other problem can there be greater than this one'.**"

❖

The truth of the matter ...
A bum asks a man for two dollars. The man asked, "Will you buy booze?"
The bum said, "No."
The man asked, "Will you gamble it away?"
The bum said, "No."
Then the man asked, "Will you come home with me, so my wife can see **what happens to a man who doesn't drink or gamble!"**

Let's teach him ...
One evening, a young woman came home from a date, rather sad. She told her mother, "Anthony proposed to me an hour ago."
"Then why are you so sad?" her mother asked.
"Because he also told me, he is an atheist. Mom, he doesn't even believe there's a Hell."
Her mother replied, **"Marry him anyway. Between the two of us, we'll show him just how wrong he is."**

Sharing and caring ...
Girl: "When we get married, I want to share all your worries, troubles and lighten your burden."
Boy: "It's very kind of you, darling, but I don't have any worries or troubles."
Girl: "Well, that's because we aren't married yet!"

In New York there is a sign just outside the Marriage Aid Bureau. The sign says, **"There are four secrets to a happy marriage."**
1. It is important to find a woman that cooks and cleans.
2. It is important to find a woman that makes good money.
3. It is important to find a woman that likes to have sex.
4. **It is important that these three women never meet!!**

What do men do immediately after sex?
5% fall asleep straight after
15% go to the bathroom to wash
20% roll over and light up a cigarette
60% go home to their wives!!!

Bachelor: "Is it true that men have more sense after they marry?"
Married man: "Yes, but it's too late then!!"

I was married by a judge. I should have asked for a jury.
George Burns

Keeping it secret ...
A family was having dinner on Mother's Day. For some reason the mother was unusually quiet.
Husband: "What's bothering you, dear?"
Wife: "Nothing,"
Husband: "Seriously, what's wrong?"
Wife: "Do you really want to know? I've cooked, cleaned, and fed the kids for 15 years and on Mother's Day, they don't even say as much as 'Thank you'."
Husband: "Why should they? Not once in 15 years have I gotten a Father's Day gift."
Wife: "Yes, but I'm their real mother!"

❖

Truthfully ... ?
There was a middle-aged couple that had two stunningly beautiful blonde teen-aged daughters.
They decided to try one last time for the son they always wanted. After months of trying, the wife became pregnant and sure enough, nine months later delivered a healthy baby boy.
The joyful father rushed to the nursery to see his new son. He took one look and was horrified to see the ugliest child he had ever seen. He went to his wife and said that there was no way that he could be the father of that child.
"Look at the two beautiful daughters I fathered."
Then he gave her a stern look and asked, "Have you been fooling around on me?"
The wife just smiled sweetly and said,
"Not this time dear..."

❖

Too good to be true ...
Four expectant fathers were in a Minneapolis hospital waiting room while their wives were in labour. The nurse arrived and announced to the first man, "Congratulations sir, you're the father of twins."

"What a coincidence!" the man said proudly. "I work for the Minnesota Twins baseball team."

The nurse returned in a little while and said to the second man, "You, sir, are the father of triplets."

"Wow, that's really an incredible coincidence," he answered. "I work for the 3M Corporation."

The nurse came back and turned to the third man. She announced that his wife had just given birth to quadruplets.

"I don't believe it; I work for the Four Seasons Hotel."

Meanwhile, everybody's attention turned to the fourth guy, who had just fainted, flat out on the floor. When he was finally able to speak, everyone could hear him whispering repeatedly the same phrase over and over again. **"I should have never taken that job at 7-Up. I should have never taken that job at 7-Up. I should have never taken that job at 7-Up...."**

A burglar enters a house in the middle of the night. He was interrupted when the owner awoke.

Drawing his gun, the burglar said, "Don't move or I'll shoot. I'm hunting for your money."

"Let me turn on the light," replied the victim, **"and I'll hunt with you!!"**

Husbands & Wives

The benefits of recycling ...

A wife arriving home after a shopping trip was horrified to find her husband in bed with a lovely, young, thing.

Just as she was about to storm out of the house, her husband stopped her with these words,

"Before you leave, I want you to hear how this all came about."

"Driving home, I saw this poor, tired, young girl, so I offered her a ride.

She was hungry, so I brought her home and gave her some of the roast you had long forgotten about, in the refrigerator.

Her shoes were worn-out so I gave her a pair of your shoes that you never wear because they are out of style.

She was cold so I gave her that new birthday sweater you never use because the colour didn't suit you.

Her slacks were worn-out so I gave her a pair of yours that you don't want anymore.

Then as she was about to leave the house, she paused and asked, 'Is there anything else that your wife doesn't use anymore?'

So, here we are!!"

I haven't spoken to my wife in 18 months – I don't like to interrupt her!

It's the difference that counts ...
A man married one of a pair of identical twins. Less than a year later, he was in court filing for a divorce.
"Tell the court why you want a divorce," the judge said.
"Well, Your Honour," Dan started, "every once in a while my sister-in-law comes over for a visit, and because she and my wife are identical twins, sometimes I'd end up making love to her by mistake."
"Surely there must be some difference between the two women," the judge said.
"Exactly, Your Honour. That's why I want the divorce!!"

His turn to cry ...
This guy was describing to his friends, his silver anniversary celebration:
"It was a great celebration. We flew to the same town where we first met and got married.
We went to the same restaurant and sat at the very same table where we first had our dinner together.
We even stayed in the same hotel and occupied the very same suite we had taken on our wedding night.
In fact, everything was identical. The only difference was - **this time it was I who went into bathroom and cried!!"**

Bachelor: a man who has missed the opportunity to make some woman miserable

Who's complaining ...
A husband and wife were sitting at the breakfast table and the man was reading the ads in the paper.
He looked up and said, "Here is a great sale on tyres!"
His wife replied, "What do you want tyres for? You don't have a car."
He says, **"Do I complain when you go out and buy a new bra!"**

❖

He's all heart ...
A Golfer is playing on his own when he hits the ball into lake.
He retrieves the ball together with a bottle. He opens the bottle and a genie appears and says, "I will grant you 3 wishes, and each wish granted will be doubled for your wife."
The delighted golfer said, "Okay, I want to play better golf, so reduce my handicap by 5."
"All right" said the genie, "your wish is granted. Your handicap will be reduced by 5 and your wife's by 10"
"My second wish," said the golfer, "is to win a lottery for one million dollars."
"Done," replied the genie, "you will win one million dollars and your wife will win two million dollars."
"Now," said the golfer, **"my third wish is, please give me a mild heart attack!!"**

❖

Wife: Will you love me when I'm old and ugly?
Husband: Darling, of course I do!!

❖

It's about good timing ...
A guy sticks his head into a barbershop and asks, "How long before I can get a haircut?"
The barber looks around the shop and says, "About 2 hours." The guy leaves.
A few days later, the same guy sticks his head in the door and asks, "How long before I can get a haircut?"
The barber looks around at shop full of customers and says, "About 3 hours." The guy leaves.
This same scenario takes place several times, until one day the barber gets curious and tells his friend in the shop, "Hey, Bill, follow that guy and see where he goes. He keeps asking how long he has to wait for a haircut, but then doesn't come back."
A little while later, Bill comes back into the shop, laughing hysterically.
The barber asks, "Bill, where did he go when he left here?"
Bill looks up, tears in his eyes and says, **"Your house!"**

I take my wife everywhere, but she keeps finding her way back!

Wife: Let's go out and have some fun tonight.
Husband: Okay, but if you get home before I do, leave the hallway light on.

Surprise! Surprise!

On his 45th birthday, a guy looked forward to breakfast, expecting his wife to wish him 'Happy Birthday', and probably hand him a present too. Sadly, she didn't even say 'Good Morning'. And neither did the children.

He left for work, feeling pretty low and despondent. In his office, his secretary, Janet cheerfully greeted him, "Good Morning, Boss, Happy Birthday." He began to feel a little better.

About noon, she said, "Since it's your birthday, let's go to lunch, just you and me."

"By George," he thought. "That's the greatest thing I've heard all day." They went to a little private place in the countryside and enjoyed lunch tremendously.

After lunch, she said, "We don't really need to go back to the office, do we? Let's go to my apartment."

At her apartment, they relaxed pleasantly and she said, "Boss, if you don't mind, I think I'll go into the bedroom and slip into something more comfortable."

"Sure," he replied excitedly. She went into the bedroom and in about six minutes, she came out…., carrying a big birthday cake, followed by his wife and children. All were singing Happy Birthday… And there on the couch he sat… **with nothing on but his socks!!**

A wife asks hubby how many women he had slept with.

Husband proudly replies, **"Only you darling, with others I was awake!"**

Your money's worth ...
Larry's barn burned down and his wife, Susan, called the insurance company.
Susan told the insurance company, "We had that barn insured for fifty thousand and I want my money."
The agent replied, "Whoa there, just a minute, Susan. Insurance doesn't work quite like that. We will ascertain the value of what was insured and provide you with a new one of comparable worth."
There was a long pause before Susan replied, **"Then, I'd like to cancel the policy on my husband!"**

Wishes do come true ...
A couple is taking a stroll in a lovely meadow when they come upon a **wishing well**.
The woman leans over, makes a wish, and throws in a coin.
Her husband decides he too wants to make a wish. Unfortunately, he leans over too far and falls down into the well.
The woman stands there shaken for a moment, and then exclaims, **"Wow, it WORKS!!"**

Former President Franklin Roosevelt's wife Eleanor returned home after a full medical check up and happily said, "Darling, the doctor says that I am in perfect state of health."
Oh really," said Franklin, "And did he say anything about that big fat bum of yours?"
"No, Honey," replied Eleanor, **"Your name was never mentioned at all."**

Tea and sympathy ...
A woman accompanied her husband to the doctor's office.
After his check up, the doctor called the wife into his office alone.
He said, "Your husband is suffering from a very severe disease, combined with horrible stress. If you don't do the following, your husband will surely die."
Each morning, fix him a healthy breakfast. Be pleasant, and make sure he is in a good mood.
For lunch make him a nutritious meal he can take to work.
For dinner, prepare an especially nice meal for him.
Don't burden him with chores, as this could further his stress.
Don't discuss your problems with him; it will only make his stress worse.
Try to relax your husband in the evening by wearing sexy lingerie and give him plenty of back rubs.
Encourage him to watch some type of team sporting event on television.
In addition, most importantly make love with your husband several times a week and satisfy his every whim.
If you can do this for the next 10 months to a year, I think your husband will regain his health completely."
On the way home, the husband asked his wife, "What did the doctor say?"
"You're going to die!!" she replied.

They say a husband is very much like an old pair of shoes. **They are so comfortable that you don't feel like throwing them away.**

Balancing the pounds ...
A young man was back home visiting his folks. His mom asked him to set the table for dinner.
He opened the refrigerator and taped to the inside of the door was a sexy picture of a lovely, slender, perfectly built, scantily clad young woman.
"Mom, what's this?" He asked.
"Oh, I put that up there to remind me not to overeat," she answered.
"Is it working?" He asked.
"Yes and no," she explained. "I've lost 15 pounds, **but your dad has gained 20!"**

The best example ...
A man and his wife are watching a championship-boxing match on TV. Early in the second round, one of the fighters goes down for the count.
The husband sighs and says, "I'm so disappointed. It was all over in four minutes!"
The wife replies, **"Good. Now you know how I feel!"**

Au naturel ...
The other night, my wife and I were going out for dinner. She put on eye shadow, eyeliner, eyelashes, mascara, blusher and lipstick, then turned to me and said, **"Does this look natural?"**

Mathematically correct ...
Harold's wife bought a new line of expensive cosmetics guaranteed to make her look years younger.

After a lengthy session before the mirror applying the "miracle" products, she asked, "Darling, honestly, what age would you say I look?"

Looking her over carefully, Harold replied, "Judging from your skin, **twenty**; your hair, **eighteen**; and your figure, **twenty five**."

"Oh, you flatterer!" she gushed.

"Hey, wait a minute!" Harold interrupted. **"I haven't added them up yet!!"**

If dreams came true ...
One morning the wife woke up and told her husband, "Darling, I just dreamed that you gave me a pearl necklace for Valentine's Day. What do you think it means?"

"Honey," replied the husband, "You'll know on Valentine's Day."

On Valentine's Day, the husband came home with a small package and gave it to his wife. Delighted, she opened it to find a book entitled, **"The Meaning Of Dreams"!!**

My wife dresses to kill. She cooks the same way!
                                      Henny Youngman

Just making a point ...
A man spoke frantically into the phone, "My wife is pregnant and her contractions are only two minutes apart!"
"Is this her first child?" the doctor asked.
"No, you idiot!" the man shouted. **"This is her husband!"**

A change of roles ...
A couple just started their Lamaze class and they were given an activity requiring the husband to wear a bag of sand - to give him an idea of what it feels like to be pregnant.
The husband stood up and shrugged saying, "This doesn't feel so bad."
The instructor then dropped a pen and asked the husband to pick it up.
"You want me to pick up the pen as if I were pregnant, the way my wife would do it?" the husband asked.
"Exactly," replied the instructor.
To the delight of the other husbands, he turned to his wife and said, **"Honey, pick up that pen for me!"**

We always hold hands. If I let go, she shops!

A matter for CSI
Three weeks after her wedding day, Joanna called her minister. "Reverend," she wailed, "John and I had a DREADFUL fight!"

"Calm down, my child," said the minister, "it's not half as bad as you think. Every marriage has to have its first fight!"

"I know, I know!" cried Joanna. **"But what am I going to do with the BODY?"**

Job limitations ...
A young woman greeted the census taker.

"Good morning," said the caller, "I'm taking the census and I'd like to ask you a few quick questions.
"Occupation?"

"Homemaker," replied the woman.
"Husband's occupation?"

"Manufacturer."
"Children?"

"No," said the woman. **"Dresses!"**

Sweet secrets ...
A guy noticed that a husband married for **40 years** was still addressing his wife as, 'Darling, Honey, Sugar, Sweetheart …'

Curious, he asked this husband, "How come you still address your wife with those pet names even after 40 years of marriage?"

The husband hung his head. "To tell you the truth," he said, **"I forgot her name about ten years ago!"**

Please don't pay the ransom ...
Having gone to his secretary's apartment, Mr. Biggs was astonished to wake up and find that it was three in the morning.
"My God!" he shouted, "My wife is going to kill me!"
Unsure of how he would explain it, he ran to the nearest pay phone and called his wife.
"Honey!" he began, **"Don't pay the ransom. I escaped!"**

Did you say 'whore' or 'horse' ...
This man is sitting quietly and peacefully, reading his paper one morning, when his wife sneaks up behind him and whacks him on the back of his head with a huge frying pan.
Husband: "What was that for?"
Wife: "What was that piece of paper in your pants pocket with the name 'Daisylou' written on it?"
Husband: "Oh honey, remember two weeks ago, I went to the horse races? 'Daisylou' was the name of one of the horses I bet on."
She is appeased and goes off to work around the house. Three days later, while he is sitting in his chair reading, his wife whacks his head with the frying pan again.
Husband: "What's that for this time?"
Wife: "Your horse just called!"

Choices – the bad or the terrible first ...
Rodney sat in his attorney's office.
Lawyer: Shall I give you the bad news first, or the terrible news?
Rodney: Give me the bad news first.
Lawyer: Your wife found a picture worth half a million dollars.
Rodney: You're kidding, that's bad news? So what's the terrible news?
Lawyer: The picture is of you and your mistress.

The conjugal trail ...
"Madam," said the private detective hired by the wife, "we trailed your husband to two sexy discotheques and somebody's bachelor apartment."
"And what was that cheating husband of mine doing?" asked the woman.
"Madam," replied the detective, **"He was trailing you!"**

"My wife had a funny dream last night. She dreamed she had married a multi-millionaire."
"You're lucky," said George, **"my wife dreams that in the day time!"**

The husband who wants **a happy marriage** should learn to keep his mouth **shut** and his chequebook **open**.   Groucho Marx

The unkindest cut of all ...
"My husband and I had a very bad fight last night"
"Why, what happened?"
"Well, he was rummaging around looking for something when he discovered my birth control pills."
"So what?"
"Well, he had a vasectomy two years ago."

It's a stiff budget to live on ...
The husband came home one day and started to pack his bag.
"Where to?" asked his surprised wife."
"To the Canaries," replied the husband, "I hear there are so many women in there, they even pay a man $20 to make love to them."
Hearing this the wife started to pack too.
"And where you heading for?" asked the husband.
"I am coming with you," said the wife, **"I want to see how you can live on $40 a month."**

Singapore Broadcasting Corporation conducted a survey on the secret of a happy marriage. They interviewed a man who was married for 50 yrs. "Well," he said, "it's like this; my wife and I go out to dinner twice a week. Nice restaurant, soft music, bottle of wine, candlelight dinner and then a nice stroll under the moonlight. **She goes Tuesdays and I go Fridays.**

Who wears the panties in this house ...
The wife searched high and low for a new pair of expensive panties she had recently purchased for herself.
Unable to find it, she suspected the maid and shouted, "Where are my new panties? Have you taken them for yourself?"
"No, Madam, I have not taken them," replied the maid.
"Then where are they? I have searched the whole house. You are lying. You must have taken them for yourself."
"No, Madam I swear I have not. If you don't believe you can check with the Master. **He knows I never wear panties!"**

Caught in the act ...
Drowsing contentedly after an afternoon of passionate love-making, they suddenly hear the sound of a car pulling up outside.
Dreamily, the girl whispers, "Oh, oh, quick get moving, that's my husband."
Quick as a flash, the man jumps out of bed, rushes to the window and suddenly stops dead.
"Whaddya mean?" he bellows, **"I AM your husband!"**

We sleep in separate beds. Hers is in Florida and mine is in New York.

The cure for headaches ...
A fellow is feeling a little frisky, but true to his wife, goes home. He finds her sound asleep in the bed with her mouth wide open. He gets two aspirins and drops them in her mouth. She starts to choke, but recovers and asks, "What did you put in my mouth?"
He says, "Two aspirins."
She replies, "BUT I DON'T HAVE A HEADACHE!"
He says, **"That's all I wanted to hear...!!"**

A nice exchange ...
A husband was enjoying his morning paper when his bored wife came up to him and said, "I wish I were a newspaper so that you could hold me in your arms everyday."
The husband replied, **"Yes Dear, I too wish you were, so I could have a new one everyday!"**

Husband: Honey, where would you like to go for our anniversary?
Wife: Somewhere I haven't been in a long time!
Husband: Okay, how about the kitchen!

A housewife ran after the garbage truck, yelling, "Am I too late for the garbage?"
The driver said, **"No, jump in!"**

To have your cake and eat it too ...
A woman in a diet club was sharing her experience and lamenting that she had gained weight.
She had made her family's favourite cake over the weekend, she reported, and they'd eaten half of it at dinner.
The next day, she said, she kept staring at the other half, until finally she cut a thin slice for herself.
One slice led to another, and soon the whole cake was gone.
The woman went on to tell how upset she was with her lack of willpower, and how she knew her husband would be disappointed.
Everyone felt sad for her; until someone asked what her husband said when he found out.
She smiled. **"He never found out. I made another cake and ate half!"**

It works like magic ...
A man approached a very beautiful woman in a large supermarket and asked, "Can you talk to me for a couple of minutes?"
"Why?" she asks.
"Because I have lost my wife here in the supermarket and every time I talk to a beautiful woman, **my wife appears out of nowhere."**

For every man there is a woman, and he's lucky if his wife never finds out.

What could be worse ...
"Cash, cheque or charge?" the cashier asked after packing items the woman wished to purchase. As the woman fumbled for her wallet, the cashier noticed a remote control for a television set in her purse. "Do you always carry your TV remote?" the cashier asked.
"No," she replied, "but my husband refused to come shopping with me, so I figured **this was the most evil thing I could do to him!"**

The sleeping partner ...
Suspecting her husband of infidelity, the woman attempted to put an end to it by arousing his jealousy. "What would you say if I told you that I've been sleeping with your best friend?" she asked provocatively.
"Well," he mused, **"I'd have to say that you're a lesbian!"**

An elderly couple were celebrating the wife's centennial.
The husband went in front of the gathering and raised a toast to his wife. "Darling, may you live to be 119 years."
The surprised wife went up to him and asks, "Why not 120 years?"
"Because," said the husband**, "One year I want peace."**

Just whistle while you work ...
Two friends are having a chat at the bar and sharing their home and family life.
Said the first friend: "My wife and I have a 2 bedroom apartment. We have 2 babies and no maid. My wife sleeps with the babies in one room, while I sleep in the other."
Asked the other friend: "But what if you have an urge at night?"
"Well" replied the 1st friend, "We have a good arrangement. If I get the urge during the night, I blow a soft whistle and she gets the signal and comes to my room."
"But what if your wife gets the urge?" asked the surprised friend.
"Simple," he replied, "she comes to my room, knocks on the door and asks: **Darling, did you whistle?"**

A bad night at the casino
This wife, a big gambler, would always come home late every night after her gin rummy session. One night, she came home very, very late. In order not to disturb her husband's sleep, she took off all her clothes in the living room, and with only her handbag in her hands, she tiptoed into the bedroom.
The husband was lying down, reading a book under his bedside lamp. He looked at her and said, **"My God, this time you have lost everything!!"**

He never misses a game …
Two golfers were putting on the green, near the road, when a funeral procession passed.
The hearse carrying the coffin displayed the picture of the deceased in the front.
Recognizing the face, the 1st golfer remarked: "It's Mrs. Sam. They've put the golf bag on top of her coffin. She must have been a real ardent lover of golf!"
2nd Golfer: **"No, that bag belongs to her husband. He has a game at 2.30."**

The personal touch …
"I'd like to buy some gloves for my wife," the young man said, eyeing the attractive salesgirl, "but I don't know her size."
"Will this help?" she asked sweetly, placing her hand in his.
"Oh, yes," he answered. "Her hands are just slightly smaller than yours."
"Will there be anything else?" the salesgirl queried as she wrapped the gloves.
"Now that you mention it," he replied, **"she also needs a bra and panties!"**

Judge: You admit having broken into the same dress shop **four** times. What did you steal?"
Accused: A dress for my wife, Your Honour, but she made me change it **three times**."

What you wish is what you get ...
Once some men got together to play poker one night. After about 4 hours of playing, Tim had severe chest pains and suddenly slumped over. One of the gamblers who happened to be a doctor, examined him, and to everyone's shock, poor Tim had died of a heart attack.
All his friends didn't know how to break the news to his wife. Finally Johnny said: "I can be diplomatic about it and break the news gently!"
Johnny rang the bell at Tim's house, and when his wife answered the door, he calmly said to her: "Tim just gambled with us and lost 1,000 dollars!"
When Tim's wife heard this she said: "Tell him to just drop dead!"
Johnny answered: **"That's exactly what he did!"**

The new Night golf-clubs ...
Wife to husband: "What's your excuse for coming home at this time of the night?"
Husband to wife: "Golfing with friends, my dear."
Wife to husband: "What? At 2 a.m.?!"
Husband to wife: "Yes, We used night clubs!"

She put on a mudpack and looked great for two days. Then the mud fell off!

Gentlemen prefer 'balds' too ...
A salesman's wife was terribly suspicious. Every evening she subjected her husband to an inspection and if she found even a single hair on his coat, she created a terrible scene.
One night she found nothing so she screamed;
"NOW IT'S A BALD HEADED WOMAN"

Addendum to an epitaph ...
When her late husband's will was read, a widow learned he had left the bulk of his fortune to another woman.
Enraged, she rushed to change the inscription on her spouse's tombstone.
"Sorry, lady," said the stonecutter. "I inscribed **'Rest in Peace'** on your orders. I can't change it now."
"Very well," she said grimly. "Just add, **'Until We Meet Again.'!"**

Doctor: "There is no need to worry about your wife; you'll have a different woman when she gets back from the hospital."
Anxious husband: "And what if she finds out!"

Outdoor Salesman: Sir, are you the head of the house?
"Yes, I am," said the man, **"Until my wife returns from the Supermarket."**

It's easier to move a mountain ...
A man was walking along a California beach, in deep prayer to the Lord. He said, "Lord, you've promised to give me what I really wish for. Please give me a sign that you will grant my prayer."

Suddenly the sky darkened and the Lord said, "I've searched your heart and seen it to be pure. I'll grant you one wish."

The man said, "I've always wanted to go to Hawaii but I'm deathly afraid of flying and I get very seasick in boats. Could you build a bridge so that I can drive there whenever I want?" The Lord laughed and said, "That's impossible! Think of the logistics! How would the supports ever reach the bottom of Pacific? Your request is very materialistic and disappointing. Take a little more time and make another one."

After much thought, the man said, "I've been married 4 times. My wives always said that I was insensitive to their needs. So I **wish** I could understand woman."

To which the Lord replied**... "You want 2 or 4 lanes on that bridge?"**

When looks don't count ...
After completing his examination, the doctor took her husband aside. "I don't like the looks of your wife at all."

"Me neither, Doc," said the husband. "But she's a good cook and the kids seem to like her."

47

The regular 'sun-downer' ...
Husband comes home from an exhausting day at work, plops down on the couch in front of the television, and tells his wife Cathy, "Get me a beer **before it starts**."
The wife sighs and gets him a beer. Fifteen minutes later, husband says, "Get me another beer **before it starts**."
Wife looking cross fetches another beer and slams it down next to him. Husband finishes that beer. A few minutes later he again says, "Quick, get me another beer, it's **going to start** any minute."
Wife is now furious. She yells at him, "Is that all you're going to do tonight? Drink beer and sit in front of that TV? You're nothing but a lazy, drunken, fat slob, and furthermore...
Husband sighs and says, **"It's started!"**

A biological bloomer ...
An old man married a 20-year-old blonde. He consulted the doctor to give something to pep him up.
The Doctor gave him a jab from the glands of a sexy monkey. It worked. The wife delivered the baby.
The Old man asked, "Doc, is it a boy or a girl?"
"I don't know. But I'll tell you as soon as it comes down from the chandelier!"

Yawn: The only time some married men ever get to open their mouth.

Once is enough ...
A well-dressed gentleman entered a classy restaurant and took a seat at the bar.
The bartender came over and asked, "What can I get you to drink, sir?"
The gentleman responded, "Nothing, thank you. I tried alcohol once, didn't like it, and never tried it again."
The bartender was a bit perplexed, but being a friendly, outgoing sort, pulled out a pack of cigarettes and offered the gentleman a cigarette. The gentleman refused, saying, "I tried smoking once, didn't like it, and never did it again. The point is, I wouldn't be in here at all, except that I'm waiting for my son."
The bartender retorted, **"Your only child, I presume!"**

Never take candy from a stranger ...
A couple walking in the park noticed a young man and woman sitting on a bench, passionately kissing.
"Why don't you do that?" said the wife.
"Honey," replied her husband, **"I don't even know that woman!"**

Husband and wife were in the midst of a violent quarrel, and the husband was losing his temper.
Husband: Be careful, you will bring out the animal in me.
Wife: So what, who is afraid of a mouse?

Even miracles have their limits ...
Grandma and Grandpa were watching a healing service on the television. The evangelist called to all who wanted to be healed to go to their television set, place one hand on the TV and the other hand on the body part where they wanted to be healed.

Grandma got up and slowly hobbled to the television set, placed her right hand on the set and her left hand on her arthritic shoulder that was causing her to have great pain.

Then Grandpa got up, went to the TV, placed his right hand on the set and his left hand on his crotch.

Grandma scowled at him and said, "I guess you just don't get it. **The purpose of doing this is to heal the sick, not to raise the dead!"**

There's nothing I wouldn't do for you ...
On his golden wedding anniversary, the old man told his friends; There's nothing I wouldn't do for my wife and there's nothing my wife wouldn't do for me. And that's how it has been for the last year - **we've done nothing for each other!!**

Every man wants a wife who is beautiful, understanding, economical, and a good cook. But the law allows only one wife.

The husband was seeing his wife off at the station. "Don't come on to the platform dear," said his wife, "it will cost you a dollar for a ticket."
"That's all right," he replied. **"It's worth more than a dollar to see you off."**

❖

A time for everything under heaven ...
Husband telling house rules to his wife: "I will eat when I want to eat; and come home when I want to."
Wife: "OK. But there will be sex at 7 pm with or without you!"

❖

A toast in the right direction ...
A woman at a party walked up to a man and told him, "If you were my husband I would poison your drink."
The man replied, **"If you were my wife I would drink it!!"**

❖

Bob: "My wife drives like lightning."
Ted: "She drives fast?"
Bob: "She hits trees!"

❖

Men and Women

Let's go shopping!

A man and a woman walk into a very posh Rodeo Drive store.

"Show the lady your finest mink!" the fellow exclaims.

So, the owner of the shop goes to the back and comes out with an absolutely gorgeous full-length coat.

As the lady tries it on, the owner discreetly whispers to the man, "Ah, sir that particular fur goes for $65,000."

"No problem! I'll write you a cheque!"

"Very good, sir." says the shop owner. "Today is Saturday. You may come by on Monday to pick it up, after the cheque has cleared."

So the man and the woman leave. On Monday, the fellow returns. The storeowner is outraged. "How dare you show your face in here? There wasn't a single penny in your checking account!!"

"I just had to come by," grinned the guy, "to thank you for the most wonderful weekend of my life!!"

Communication

When two men are talking to each other, they are talking about themselves.

When two women are talking to each other, they are talking about a third one!

Life after marriage
A woman candidate was making a house-to-house call to her constituency. "Good morning, Mrs. Jones, I am the independent candidate. May I hope that your husband will support me?"
"Support you?" said Mrs. Jones, **"Why he hasn't supported me for the last three years!"**

Staying alive
An 85-year-old widow went on a blind date with a 90-year-old man. When she returned to her daughter's house later that night, she seemed upset.
"What happened, Mother?" the daughter asked
"I had to slap his face three times!"
"You mean he got fresh?"
"No," she answered. **"I thought he was dead!"**

Venus and Mars
An English professor wrote the words,
'Woman without her man is nothing,' on the blackboard and directed the students to punctuate it correctly.
The men wrote: 'Woman, without her man, is nothing.'
The women wrote: 'Woman! Without her, man is nothing!'

The perfect man

A group of girlfriends on vacation see a five-storey hotel with a sign that reads: **'For Women Only'** and they decide to go in.

The bouncer, a very attractive guy, explains to them how it works. "We have five floors. Go up floor by floor, and once you find what you are looking for, you can stay there. It's easy to decide since each floor has a sign telling you what's inside."

So they start going up, and on the first floor the sign reads: **'All the men on this floor are short and plain.'**

The friends laugh, and without hesitation move on to the next floor.

The sign on the second flo*or* reads: **'All the men here are short and handsome.'**

Still, this isn't good enough.

They reach the third floor and the sign reads: **'All the men here are tall and plain.'**

They still want better. Knowing there are still two floors left, they keep going.

On the fourth floor, the sign is perfect**: 'All the men here are tall and handsome.'**

The women get excited and are about to go in when they realize that there is still one floor left.

Wondering what they are missing, they head up to the fifth floor. There they find a sign that reads:

'There are no men here. This floor was built only to prove that there is no way to please a woman.'

Horizontal cha-cha ...

Three cars were parked in a dark lane. A traffic cop, passing by, saw arms and legs moving inside the vehicles. He approached the 1st car, knocked on the window and asked, "What's happening down there?"

The window of the car rolled down and the woman inside replied, "It's all right officer, the radio is on and we're doing the Rock and Roll."

The cop went to the 2nd car, and enquired, "What are both of you doing inside?"

The window rolled down and a woman inside replied, "It's all right officer, the radio is on and we're doing the Twist."

The cop then walked to the 3rd car, and said, "And I suppose your radio is on and you are both doing the BOZANOVA."

The woman rolled down the window and said, "No, I am doing the **BOSS A FAVOUR!"**

The kick off ...

Two guys are talking about their boss' upcoming wedding.

One says, "It's ridiculous, he's rich but he's 92 years old, and she's just 25! What kind of a wedding is that?"

The other says, "Well, we have a name for that. We call it a **football wedding**."

The first asks, "What's a football wedding?"

The other says, **"She's waiting for him to kick off!!"**

Brains vs. brawn
Eleven people were hanging on a rope under a helicopter, ten men and one woman. The rope was not strong enough to carry them all, so they decided that one had to leave, otherwise they were all going to fall.

They were not able to name that person, until the woman gave a very touching speech. She said that she would voluntarily let go of the rope, because as a woman she was used to giving up everything for her husband and kids, or for men in general, without ever getting anything in return.

As soon as she finished her speech, all the men started clapping their hands...

The five ages of women
How women differ at each age -
At age 8 - You take her to bed and tell her a story.
At age 18 - You tell her a story and then take her to bed.
At age 28 - You don't need to tell her any story; just take her to bed.
At age 38 - She tells you a story and takes you to bed.
At age 48 - You tell her a story to avoid going to bed.

If you want a committed man, look in a mental hospital!

The last word ...
A wife takes her husband's fully equipped fishing boat out to read her book. Along comes a game warden in his boat. He pulls up alongside the woman and says, "Good morning Ma'am. What are you doing?"
"Reading a book," she replies.
"You're in a restricted fishing area," he informs her.
"I'm sorry officer, but I'm not fishing, I'm reading."
"Yes, but you have all the equipment. I'll have to take you in and write you up."
"If you do that, I'll have to charge you with sexual assault," says the woman.
"But I haven't even touched you," says the game warden.
"That's true, but you have all the equipment."

MORAL: Never argue with a woman who reads. **It's likely she can also think!**

Discussion technique
A woman has the last word in any argument.
Anything a man says after that is the beginning of a new argument.

Man: If I could see you naked, I'd die happy.
Woman: If I saw you naked, I'd probably die laughing.

Between the sheets

A man and a woman who have never met before find themselves in the same sleeping carriage of a train. After the initial embarrassment, they both manage to get to sleep; the man on the top bunk, the woman on the lower.

In the middle of the night the man leans over and says, "I'm sorry to bother you Miss, but I'm awfully cold and I was wondering if you could possibly pass me another blanket."

The woman leans out and with a glint in her eye said "I've got a better idea ... let's pretend we're married."

"Why not," smiles the man, delightedly.

"Good," she replies. **"Get up and go get your own blanket."**

A woman was painting the walls of her apartment.

As the paint was dripping all over her dress, she removed all her clothes and resumed painting.

Soon after there was a knock on the door.

"Who is that?" she asked.

"I am a blind man." came the reply.

She opened the door. The guy looked at her and said, "Wow! You are a very beautiful woman."

"Hey, I thought you said you were a blind man!!!"

"Yes, I am. Where would you like the blinds to be fixed?"

Running after women never hurt anybody. It's the catching that does the damage.

What a man wants
An architect, an artist, and a scientist were discussing whether it was better to spend time with the wife or a mistress.

The architect said he enjoyed time with his wife, building a solid foundation for an enduring relationship.

The artist said he enjoyed time with his mistress, because of the passion and mystery he found there.

The scientist said, "I like both. If you have a wife and a mistress, they will each assume you are spending time with the other woman, and **you can go to the lab and get some work done.**"

When a woman suffers in silence, it means her phone is out order.

Why women over 40 are the greatest. The **look swell** and they are **built well**. They **seldom yell**, they **never tell** and they are **grateful as hell**.

Man: Haven't I seen you some place before?
Woman: Yes, that's why I don't go there anymore.

Who's in control ...
Three guys are chatting in a pub. Two of them are talking about the amount of control they have over their wives, while the third remains quiet.
After a while the first man turns to the third and says, "Well, what about you, what sort of control you have over your wife?"
The third fellow says, "Huh, just the other night my wife came to me on her hands and knees."
The first two guys were amazed. "What happened then?" they asked.
"She said, 'Get out from under the bed you coward'!!"

A woman went to see the Doctor for the second time.
The doctor looked at her and said, "Why, you look pale and totally exhausted. Did you take my advice to **take three meals** everyday?"
"Oh!" said the woman, **"I thought you said "MALES"**

Marriage is when a man and woman become as one. The trouble starts when they try to decide which one.

Man: I would go to the end of the world for you.
Woman: But would you stay there?

Men are ... Women are ...

If a man goes on a seven-day trip, he'll pack five days worth of clothes and will wear some things twice;
If a woman goes on a seven-day trip, she'll pack 21 outfits because she doesn't know what she'll feel like wearing each day.

❖

Men are like Government bonds. They take so long to mature.

❖

Behind every successful man stands a woman. Behind every unsuccessful man stand two women.

❖

Q: Why are hurricanes normally named after women?
A: When they come, they're wild and wet, but when they go, they take your house and car with them.

❖

Men are like Bank Accounts. Without a lot of money, they don't generate much interest.

❖

Behind every successful man stands a woman. Behind that woman stands a wife.

❖

He says... She says...

He: I'm a photographer I've been looking for a face like yours!
She: I'm a plastic surgeon. I've been looking for a face like yours!!!

❖

He: Hi! Didn't we go on a date once? Or was it twice?
She: Must've been once. I never make the same mistake twice!!!

❖

He: Can I have your name?
She: Why, don't you already have one?

❖

He: What would you say if I asked you to marry me?
She: Nothing. I can't talk and laugh at the same time!!!

❖

He: Your face must turn a few heads!
She: And your face must turn a few stomachs!!!

❖

He: I think I could make you very happy
She: Why? Are you leaving?

❖

Parents and Kids

Choose your looks ...
Father: "When you go back to your Mom tonight, give her this envelope and tell her that since you are now 18, this is the LAST cheque she'll ever see from me for child support. Then, stand back and watch the expression on her face."
Daughter: "Mom, Dad asked me to give you this envelope. He said to tell you that since I'm now 18, this is the LAST child support payment he'll ever have to make to you. Now I'm supposed to stand back and watch the expression on your face."
Mother: "Next time you visit your father, tell him that after 18 years I have decided to inform him that he's not your father. **Then, stand back and watch the expression on HIS face!!"**

True to life ...
A little boy returned from school and enthusiastically announced that he'd gotten a part in a play.
Father: "And what part would you be playing son?"
Son: "I play a man who's been married for twenty years."
Father: "That's great, son. Keep up the good work and before you know it they'll be giving you **a speaking part!!"**

When two's company, three's the result!

63

The colour of love
Attending a wedding for the first time, a little girl whispered to her mother, "Why is the bride dressed in white?"

"Because white is the colour of happiness and today is the happiest day of her life," her mother tried to explain, keeping it simple.

The child thought about this for a moment, and then said, **"So, why's the groom wearing black!!"**

Making the grade
Joey walked into his dad's study while his dad was working on the computer.

"Dad," said Joey, "Remember when you told me you'd give me twenty dollars if I passed my math test?" Dad nodded. **"Well,"** said Joey, **"the good news is that I just saved you twenty bucks!"**

Daddy's trick
The little boy greeted his grandmother with a hug and said, "I'm so happy to see you Grandma. Now maybe Daddy will do the trick he has been promising us."

The grandmother was curious.

"What trick is that dear?" she asked.

The little boy replied, "I heard Daddy tell Mommy that **he would climb the walls if you came to visit us again!"**

Sex education

Brody came home from school one day and asked his mom, "Mom, what is sex?"

His mom was flustered, but she knew this day would come, and decided to be honest.

She spent the next hour explaining to her son about the birds and the bees, and where babies came from. When she was done her son smiled, pulled a questionnaire out of his pocket and pointed to the word sex. **"That's cool, but how am I supposed to get it all in this little box next to the F and the M?!"**

Daddy's little boy

One summer evening, during a violent thunderstorm, a mother was tucking her small boy into bed. She was about to turn off the light when he asked with a tremor in his voice, "Mommy, will you sleep with me tonight?"

The mother smiled and gave him a reassuring hug. "I can't dear," she said, "I have to sleep with Daddy."

A long silence was broken at last by a shaken little voice saying, **"The big sissy!!"**

Daddy's little helper

Trying to come to the aid of his Father, who was stopped by an officer for speeding, the six-year-old boy sitting behind piped up, **"Yeah? Well, if we were speeding, so were you!"**

Keeping your cool

The young father, pushing a baby carriage, seemed quite unperturbed by the wails emerging from it. "Easy now, Terry," he said quietly, "control yourself, keep calm." Another howl rang out, "Now, now Terry," murmured the parent, "Keep your temper."

A young mother passing by remarked, "I must congratulate you! You know how to speak to a child."

"The child's not the problem," he said, **"MY name's Terry!!"**

In a general knowledge class, the teacher asked, "Johnny, 4 birds are sitting on a tree, 1 is shot, how many are left?"

"None" replied Johnny, "because the others flew away."

The teacher said, "Johnny, the answer is 3, **but I like your thinking**."

Johnny then sought permission of the teacher to ask her a question, which she readily agreed.

"Teacher, there are three women all eating ice-cream cones. One is biting, one licking & one sucking. Which one is married?"

The teacher blushed but replied, "The one licking the ice-cream."

"No, Teacher" replied Johnny, **"the answer is 'THE ONE WEARING A RING'. But I like your thinking."**

Out of the mouths of babes ...
A man comes home from work with his little daughter.
Little girl: "Dad, I saw you in your office with your secretary. Why do you call her **doll**?"
Feeling his wife's gaze upon him, the man explains: "Well, honey, my secretary is a very hard-working girl. She types like you wouldn't believe, she knows the computer system and is very efficient."
Little girl: "Oh, I thought it was because she closed her eyes when you laid her down on the couch!"

There once was a cat ...
Little Tim was in the backyard filling in a hole. His neighbour peered over the fence interested in what the cheeky-faced youngster was doing. He politely asked, "What are you doing down there, Tim?"
"My goldfish died," replied Tim tearfully, without looking up, "and I've just buried him."
The concerned neighbour said, "That's an awfully big hole for a goldfish, isn't it?"
Tim patted down the last heap of earth and then replied, **"That's because he's inside your cat!"**

Office: a place where you can relax after your strenuous day at home!

When grades do matter....
A Mom is driving a little girl to her friend's house for a play date.
"Mommy," the little girl asks, "how old are you?"
"Honey, it's not polite to ask a lady her age," the mother says.
"OK," the little girl says, "How much do you weigh?"
"Now dear," the mother says, "this is also a personal question."
Undaunted, the little girl asks, "Why did you and Daddy get a divorce?"
"That's enough of questions!" and the exasperated mother walks away as the two friends begin to play.
"My Mom wouldn't tell me anything," the little girl says to her friend.
"Well," says the friend, "just look at her driver's license. It is like a report card, it has everything on it."
Later that night the little girl says to her mother, "I know that you are 39 years and weigh 140 pounds."
The mother is absolutely surprised and asks, "How did you find that out?"
"And," the little girl says triumphantly, "I know why you and Daddy got a divorce."
"Oh really?" the mother asks. "Why?"
"Because you got an F in sex!!"

Children in backseats cause accidents.
Accidents in backseats cause children.

Family reunions
An elderly man in Phoenix calls his son in New York and says, "I hate to ruin your day, but I have to tell you that your mother and I are getting a divorce; 45 years of misery is enough."

"Pop, what are you talking about?" the son screams.

"We're sick of each other," said the father, "and I'm tired of talking about this, so you call your sister in Chicago and tell her," and he hangs up.

Frantic, the son calls his sister, who explodes on the phone. "Like hell they're getting a divorce!"

She calls Phoenix immediately, and screams at her father, "You are NOT getting divorced. Don't do a single thing until my brother and I get there. DO YOU HEAR ME?" and she hangs up.

The father hangs up his phone too, and turns to his wife. **"Okay,"** he says, **"they're coming for Thanksgiving. Now what do we tell them for Christmas!!"**

In a children's General Knowledge Class, little Johnny asked his teacher.

"Is it possible for a six years old girl to get pregnant?"

"No, of course not, Johnny." replied the teacher.

Johnny then nudged the girl sitting next to him and whispered, **"See I told you there is nothing to worry about."**

They say children brighten up a home. It's true. They never turn off the lights.

Filling the empty space?
Emily, a little girl, complaining to her mother, wanted to know why her stomach hurt.
Her mother replied, "That's because it's empty. Maybe you should try putting something in it."
The next day, the pastor was over at Emily's family's house for lunch. He mentioned that he had a migraine so his head hurt, to which Emily immediately replied, "**That's because it's empty. Maybe you should try putting something in it!!**"

Sunday school teacher asked her pupils, "Now, children, do you all say your prayers at night?"
A little boy answered: "My Mommy says my prayers."
"I see," said the teacher, "and what does your Mother say?"
Replied the little boy: **"THANK GOD HE'S IN BED!"**

A woman gave birth to a baby boy. She told her friend. "Doesn't he look like his father?"
And her friend said, "He sure does, but don't worry. **As he grows older he will change for the better!**"

With children, you spend the first 2 years of their life teaching them **to walk and talk**. Then you spend the next 16 telling them **to sit down and shut up!**

Grammatically correct
Little Johnny's Mother had been away for a week at a sales convention. When she returned home, she was anxious to hear about his week.
"Well, one night we had thunderstorm, and I was scared, so Daddy and me slept together," her son said.
"Johnny!" said the boy's young nanny, "Don't you mean Daddy and I?"
"No!" replied Johnny, **"That was Thursday; I'm talking about Monday night."**

When the cat's away ...
A travelling salesman rings the doorbell and ten year old little Johnny answers, holding a beer-can and smoking a fat cigar.
The salesman says, "Little boy, is your mother home?"
Little Johnny taps his ash on the carpet and says,
"What the hell do you think!!"

A mother takes her little boy to the zoo. They come across a cage with two lions; a male and a female.
Curious, the boy asks, "Mummy, how do lions make love?"
Mother replied, **"I don't know, son, all your Daddy's friends are Rotarians."**

The new baby
Little Johnny's new baby brother was screaming up a storm.
Johnny: "Where did we get him, Mom?"
Mother: "He came from heaven, Johnny."
Johnny: "WOW! I can see why they threw him out!"

Mommy's smart answer
Little Johnny was eating breakfast one morning and got to thinking about things.
"Mommy, Mommy, why has Daddy got so little hair on his head?" he asked his mother.
"He thinks a lot," replied his mother.
Johnny thought for a second and asked, **"So why do you have so much hair!!"**

"Dad, can you write in the dark?"
"I think so, son. What is it you want me to write?"
"Your name on this report card!"

Genes
Husband: "You know dear, our son got his brains from me."
Wife: **"I think he did, I still have mine with me!!"**

How'd he get there?
One day, an old country doctor went way out to an isolated farm to deliver a baby. It was so far out that the house didn't even have electricity. On arrival, the doctor found that there was no one home except the labouring mother and her 5-year-old child. He instructed the child to hold a lantern high so he could see, while he helped the woman deliver the baby. The mother pushed and after a little while, the doctor lifted the newborn baby by the feet and spanked him on the bottom to get him to take his first breath.

The doctor then asked the 5-year-old what he thought of the baby.

The little boy responded: **"He shouldn't have crawled in there in the first place. Spank him again!"**

Minister to the little boy: Do you say a prayer before you eat?
Little boy: No, sir, my mother is a good cook.

If you have a lot of tension, and you get a headache, follow what it says on the aspirin bottle: **'Take two aspirin' and 'Keep away from children.'**

Wrong number ...
A teenage girl had been talking on the phone for about half an hour, and then she hung up.
"Wow!" said her father, "That was short. You usually talk for two hours. What happened?"
"Wrong number..." replied the girl.

It runs in the family
A young man goes to see a psychiatrist.
Young man: "I wanted to see you because I think I'm gay."
Doctor: "Oh, and what makes you think that?"
Young man: "Well, my grandfather was gay, and so was my father."
Doctor: "That doesn't mean you're gay. We don't believe that homosexuality is hereditary."
Young man: "Maybe not, but my two brothers are also gay."
Doctor: "Really?"
Young man: "That's right. And so are my two uncles and my cousin Bill."
Doctor: "That IS uncanny. Tell me, isn't there anyone in your family who likes having sex with women?"
Young man: "Yes, sir, my sister!!"

Who wears the pants ...
The teacher asked a 5-year-old girl what her father does, and she replied, **"Whatever my Mom tells him to!!"**

Bargaining power
It was painfully evident to the indignant Mother that all was not well with her attractive daughter. To her pointed questions, the girl tearfully admitted that motherhood was approaching, and that a close friend of the family was responsible.

With fire in her eyes, the Mother drove over to the friend's house and confronted him. The man readily admitted his guilt. "But I have a very good reason." the soon-to-be dad said. "I doubt I'll ever get married, and I wanted an heir to leave my fortune to. If your daughter presents me with a daughter, I'll give her $500,000. If she bears me a son, I'll make it a million."

Hearing this, the distraught Mother was silent for a while. Then, finally, she gave her reply.

"Now see here," said the Mother, **"that's totally unacceptable. If it's a miscarriage, will you at least give her another chance?"**

Cheaper by the dozen
A woman drove a mini-van filled with a dozen screaming kids through the mall parking lot, looking for a space to park. Obviously frazzled, she coasted through a stop sign.

"Hey, lady, have you forgotten how to stop?" yelled an irate man.

She rolled down her window and yelled back, **"What makes you think these are all mine?"**

Mothers-In-Law

A man's best friend

Once a guy came across a strange funeral procession. One man was walking right in front, pulling a small terrier. Behind him was a small truck carrying 2 coffins. Behind this truck were 40 men lined up in single file. Yes, SINGLE FILE! Really curious, he asked the man with the dog, "Excuse me, is this a funeral?"
"Yes, it is for my wife and my mother-in-law."
"I am sorry. They died together?"
"Well, this small dog attacked my poor wife. He killed her! My poor mother-in-law tried to save her. He killed her too."
"Gee, you mean this small dog killed your mother-in-law?!!"
"Yes, I am afraid so."
Suddenly a strange idea came to his mind.
"Do you think I can borrow this small dog for a couple of hours after the funeral, please?"
"No problem. **You see those guys at the back? They're ahead of you. Wait your turn!!**"

In the nick of time

When the husband returned home from office his wife said "Darling, this morning the big clock fell off the wall and, if it had come down a moment sooner, my mother would have been hit."
"God " said the man.**" That clock has always been slow!!"**

The plot
One year, a guy bought his mother-in-law a cemetery plot as a Christmas gift. The following year, he didn't buy her a gift. So when she asked him why, he replied, **"Well, you still haven't used the gift I bought you last year!!"**

Life after death
A guy goes on vacation to the Holy Land with his wife and mother-in-law. The mother-in-law dies. They go to an undertaker who explains that they can ship the body home but that it'll cost over $5000, whereas they can bury her in the Holy Land for only $150.
The guy says, "We'll ship her home."
The undertaker asks, "Are you sure? That's an awfully big expense and we can do a very nice burial here."
The guy says, "Look, 2000 years ago they buried a guy here and three days later he rose from the dead. **I just can't take that chance!"**

Keeping healthy
My mother-in-law started walking five miles a day when she was 60.
She's 97 today and we don't know where she is.

Mother-in-law: A guest you never invited.

Maids – the paid help ...

A woman suspects her husband is cheating on her. One day, she dials her home and a strange woman answers who says she's the maid
Woman: "We don't have a maid."
Maid: "I was hired this morning by the man of the house."
Woman: "Well, this is his wife. Is he there?"
Maid: "He is upstairs in the bedroom with someone whom I think is his wife."
Angry woman: "Listen, would you like to make $50,000?"
Maid: "What will I have to do?"
Woman: "I want you to get my gun from the desk, and shoot the jerk and the witch he's with."
The maid puts the phone down; the woman hears footsteps and the gunshots.
Maid: "What do I do with the bodies?"
Woman: "Throw them in the swimming pool."
Maid (Puzzled): "But there's no pool here."
A long pause …
Woman: "Is this 6339 8023?!!"

Love–O-Meter
During a heated spat over finances the husband said, "Well, if you'd learn to cook and were willing to clean this place, **we could fire the maid**."
The wife, fuming, shot back, "Oh yeah??? Well, if you'd learn how to make love, **we could fire the chauffeur and the gardener!!"**

Between the sheets
A rich Beverly Hills woman got very angry with her housekeeper. After a long list of stinging remarks about her work, she dismissed her.

The housekeeper couldn't allow such abuse to go unanswered and replied, "Your husband considers me a better housekeeper and cook than you, Madam."

"I suppose my husband told you that?" replied the woman.

"Yes, he did. And moreover," the angry housekeeper continued, "I am better in bed than you!"

"And I suppose my husband told you that, too?" asked the woman.

"No, Madam," said the maid**. "The mailman did!!"**

"How come your husband bought you that expensive new golf bag?"
"I caught him fooling with the maid."
"How dreadful! Did you fire her?"
"No, I still need some new clubs."

Mistress: Alice, did you clean the refrigerator, today?
Maid: Yes, Ma'am, and everything was delicious.

Faith – fully yours

The way to go ...
An old preacher was dying. He asked his banker and his lawyer, both church members, to come to his home.

As they entered the room, the preacher held out his hands and motioned for them to sit on each side of the bed. Then, he grasped their hands, sighed contentedly, smiled, and stared at the ceiling.

Both the banker and lawyer were touched and flattered but also puzzled, that the preacher asked them to be with him during his final moments.

Finally, the banker said, "Preacher, why did you ask us to come?"

The old preacher mustered up his strength and then said weakly, **"Jesus died between two thieves, and that's how I want to go!!"**

The road to heaven
The pastor was talking to a group of young children about being good and going to heaven.

At the end of his talk, he asked, "Where do you want to go?"

"Heaven!" they all piped up.

"And what do you have to do to get there?"
"Be dead!"

It's how you say it ...
A guy was smoking while saying prayers. His shocked friend asked, "Tell me how did the priest allow you to smoke while praying, when he refused to permit me."
"What did you ask?" enquired his friend.
"Can I smoke while I am praying?" replied his friend.
"No wonder he refused you, because I asked the priest, **'Can I pray while I am smoking?' and he said, 'Yes'!!"**

❖

Pinocchio's all ...
A minister told his congregation, "Next week I plan to preach about the sin of lying. To help you understand my sermon, I want you all to read Mark 17."
The following Sunday, as he prepared to deliver his sermon, the minister asked for a show of hands.
He wanted to know how many had read Mark 17.
Every hand went up. The minister smiled and said, **"Mark has only sixteen chapters. I will now proceed with my sermon on the sin of lying!!"**

❖

A Sunday school teacher asked her class why Joseph and Mary took Jesus with them to Jerusalem.
A small child replied: **"They couldn't get a baby-sitter."**

❖

The wages of sin ...
A drunk got on a bus one day and sat down next to a priest. The drunk's shirt was stained, his face was covered with red lipstick and he had half a bottle of whisky sticking out of his pocket.
After reading a page in his newspaper, he asked the priest, "Father what causes arthritis?"
"Mister, it's caused by loose living, being with cheap wicked women, too much alcohol and contempt for your fellow man".
"Well I'll be damned", muttered the drunk.
The priest, thinking about what he said turned to the man and apologized. "I'm sorry son; I didn't mean to come on so strong. How long have you had arthritis?"
"I don't, Father, I was just reading in the paper that the Pope has arthritis!!"

The new minister was talking to the oldest inhabitant.
"I am 97 years old, sir, and I haven't an enemy in the world," said the aged one.
"That is a beautiful thought," said the clergyman approvingly.
"Yes sir," was the answer. **"I'm thankful to say that I've outlived them all!!"**

If your life is in darkness, don't despair. Just pray. After praying, if your life is still in darkness, don't be stupid; **go switch on the light!**

Skinny-dipping
A minister, a priest, and a rabbi went for a hike on a very hot day. When they came upon a small, secluded lake, they took off all their clothes and jumped into the water. Refreshed, the trio decided to pick a few berries while enjoying their "freedom."

As they were crossing an open area, along came a group of ladies from town. The men ran for cover, with the minister and priest covering their privates and the rabbi covering his face.

After the ladies were gone and the men had retrieved their clothes, the minister asked the rabbi why he covered his face and not his privates. The rabbi replied, **"I don't know about you, but in MY congregation, it's my face they would recognize!!"**

Some things never change ...
A one-dollar bill met a 20-dollar bill and said, "Hey, where have you been? I haven't seen you around here much."

The twenty answered, "I've been hanging out at the casinos, went on a cruise and did the rounds of the ship, back to the United States for a while, went to a couple of baseball games, to the mall, that kind of stuff. How about you?"

The one-dollar bill said, **"You know, same old stuff, church, church, church!!"**

Who's who ...
A priest and a minister walked into a bar. After sitting down, ordering and little small talk, the priest said, "Have you noticed there are no women in this bar?" Pausing for a moment he continues, "I think we're in a gay bar."

A man approached and tried to flirt with the priest. The priest was dumbfounded, and didn't know what to do. So the minister leaned over and whispered something into the man's ear. The man nodded and walked away.

Relieved, the priest said, "Thanks. What did you tell him?"

The minister replied, **"I just told him we're on our honeymoon!!"**

A preacher visits an elderly woman from his congregation. As he sits on the couch he notices a small bowl of peanuts on the coffee table.

"Mind if I have a few?" he asks.

"No, not at all," the woman replies and pushes the bowl closer. They chat for an hour and as the preacher stands to leave, he realises that instead of eating just a few peanuts, he has emptied the bowl.

"I'm terribly sorry for eating all the peanuts; I just meant to have a few."

"That's all right," the woman replied. **"Ever since I lost my teeth, all I can do is suck off the chocolate."**

Looking for Jesus
A drunk stumbles across a baptismal service on a Sunday afternoon down by the river. He walks into the water and stands next to the preacher.
The minister notices the old drunk and says, "Mister, are you ready to find Jesus?" The drunk looks back and says, "Yes, preacher, I sure am."
The minister dunks the fellow under the water and pulls him right back up.
"Have you found Jesus?" the preacher asks.
"Nooo, I haven't!" said the drunk.
The preacher then dunks him under for quite a bit longer, brings him up, and says, "Now, brother, have you found Jesus?"
"Noooo, I have not, Reverend."
The preacher, in disgust, holds the man under for at least 30 seconds this time, brings him out of the water, and says in a harsh tone, "For the grace of God! Have you found Jesus yet?"
The old drunk wipes his eyes and says, **"Are you sure this is where he fell in?"**

It's not unusual
Late one night at the insane asylum, an inmate shouted, "I am Napoleon!"
Another one said, "How do you know?"
The first inmate said, "God told me!"
A voice from another room shouted, **"I did not!!"**

Answer to a prayer ...
An anxious lady approached her priest for advice.
Lady: Father, I have a problem. I have two female talking parrots, but they only know how to say one thing. 'Hi, we're prostitutes. Want to have some fun?'
Priest: "That's terrible! But I have a solution. Bring your two female parrots over to my house and I will put them with my two male talking parrots that I taught to pray and read the bible. My parrots will teach them to stop saying that terrible phrase and your female parrots will learn to praise and worship."
Lady: "Thank you, Father."
The next day the woman brought her female parrots to the priest's house. His two male parrots were holding rosary beads and praying in their cage. The lady put her two female parrots in with the male parrots.
Immediately, the female parrots said, "Hi, we're prostitutes, want to have some fun?"
The male parrot looked over at the other male parrot and exclaimed, **"Put the beads away. Our prayers have been answered!!"**

Minister: Why don't you come to church now, Bill?
Bill: For three reasons. First, I don't like your theology; second, I don't like your singing; **and third, it was in your church that I first met my wife.**

The VIP ...
The Pope just finished a tour of the East Coast and was going to the airport in a limousine. Since he'd never driven a limo, he asked the chauffeur if he could drive for a while. The reluctant chauffeur changed places with him and got into the back of the limo.

Once on the highway, the Pope hit 90 mph to see what the limo could do. Suddenly, he noticed the blue light of the State Patrol in his side mirror, so he pulled over.

The trooper approached the limo, peered in through the windows, and then said, "Just a moment please, I need to call in."

The trooper called and told the chief that he had pulled up a very important person for speeding. "How do I handle this, chief?" asked the trooper."

"Is it the Governor?" questioned the chief.

"No! This guy is even more important!"

"Is it the President?" asked the chief.

"No! Someone even more important!"

"Well, who the heck is it?" screamed the chief.

"I don't know, chief," replied the trooper, **"but he's got the Pope as his chauffeur!!"**

Sign outside the Church:
"Don't let worry kill, the church can help."

87

In true spirit ...
The minister of a city church enjoys a drink now and then, but his passion is peach brandy. One of his congregants usually gives him a bottle for Christmas.

When the minister went to visit his friend at Christmas, he was not disappointed but his friend told him that, in return, he had to thank him for the peach brandy from the pulpit the next Sunday.

The next Sunday the minister suddenly remembered that he had to make a public announcement to thank his friend. His friend sat in the church with a grin on his face, waiting to see the minister's embarrassment.

The minister climbed into the pulpit and said, "Before we begin, I have an announcement. I would very much like to thank my friend, Joe, for his kind gift of peaches ... **and for the spirit in which they were given!!**"

Anonymously yours ...
A Preacher was standing at the Pulpit giving his Sunday sermon, when a note was passed to him. The only word written on the sheet was **'FOOL'.**

Looking up at the Congregation, the preacher smiled and said "I have heard of men who write letters and forget to sign their names, but this is the first time I have seen a man **sign his name and forget to write the letter.**"

A lemon facial ...
Steve went to confession, and told the priest that he had been with 5 different women the night before, each one, another man's fiancée or wife.
The priest told our man Steve to go home, squeeze 3 lemons and 2 limes into a cup of water, and drink it.
Steve asked the priest if that would give him absolution.
The priest replied, **"No, but it should wipe that smug grin off your face!"**

❖

The 3 hymns ...
The Sunday before Christmas, a pastor appealed to his congregation to donate a little extra money to the church fund. He said that whoever gave the most would be able to pick out three hymns. After the collection, the pastor noticed that someone had donated a $1,000.
He was so excited that he announced he'd like to personally thank the person for the generous donation. A very quiet, elderly, saintly looking lady all the way in the back shyly raised her hand. The pastor asked her to come to the front to pick out three hymns. Her eyes brightened as she looked over the congregation, pointed to the three most handsome men in the pews and said, **"I'll take him and him and him!!!"**

❖

The tax rebate ...
Answering the phone, the priest was surprised to receive a call from the IRS auditor
"But we do not pay taxes," the priest said.
"It isn't you, Father, it's one of your parishioners, Sean McCullough. He indicates on his tax return that he gave a donation of $15,000 to the church last year. Is this, in fact, the truth?"
The priest smiled broadly. "The check hasn't arrived yet, but **I'm sure I'll have it when I remind dear Sean!!"**

Heaven or earth
Father Murphy walked into a pub and said to the first man he met, "Do you want to go to heaven?"
The man replied, "I do Father."
The priest said, "Then stand over there against the wall."
Next, the priest asked a second man, "Do you want to go to heaven?"
"Certainly, Father," was the man's reply.
Then he asked the third man who replied, "No, I don't, Father."
The priest said, "You mean to tell me that when you die you don't want to go to heaven?"
"Oh, you mean when I die." responded the third man, **"I thought you were getting a group together to go right now!!"**

The joys of sex ...
A minister gave a talk on sex to the Lions Club. When he got home, he couldn't tell his wife that he had spoken on sex, so he said he had discussed horseback riding with the members.

A few days later, she ran into some of the men at the shopping centre and the men complemented her on the speech her husband had made.

She said: "Yes I heard. I was surprised about the subject matter, as he has only tried it twice. **The first time he got so sore he could hardly walk and the second time he fell off!!"**

❖

Do you know the way ... ?
The Rev. Billy Graham tells of a time early in his career when he arrived in a small town to preach a sermon. Wanting to mail a letter, he asked a young boy where the post office was. When the boy told him, Rev. Graham thanked him and said, "If you'll come to the Baptist church this evening, you can hear me telling everyone how to get to Heaven."

"I don't think I'll be there," the boy said. **"You don't even know your way to the post office!"**

❖

SIGN AT THE CHURCH:
Come early if you want a back seat.

❖

Kindness can kill ...
Family and friends surround old Fred's hospital bed but it doesn't look good. Suddenly, he motions frantically to the pastor for something to write on. The pastor lovingly hands him a pen and a piece of paper, and Fred uses his last bit of energy to scribble a note, which he gives to the pastor, and then dies.

At Fred's funeral, the pastor realizes he's wearing the same jacket that he was wearing when Fred died. "Fred handed me a note just before he died," he says. "I haven't looked at it, but knowing Fred, I'm sure there's a word of inspiration in it for us all."

Opening the note, he reads aloud, **"Help! You're standing on my oxygen tube!!"**

A couple, desperate to conceive a child, asked their priest to pray for them.

"I'm going on a sabbatical to Rome," he replied, "and while I'm there, I'll light a candle for you."

When the priest returned three years later, he went to the couple's house and found the wife pregnant, busily attending to **two sets of twins**.

Elated, the priest wanted to congratulate her husband and asked her where he was.

"He's gone to Rome, to blow that candle out!!" came the harried reply.

A young man, excited over his first date, goes to the Pharmacy to buy a condom.

The Pharmacist asked him if he wanted one piece or a packet of six.

"Give me a packet of six" said the young man, "I am going to have great fun tonight."

When he went to pick his date in her home, the mother opened the door and invited him to join the family dinner before they leave.

At the dinner table, the young man was given the privilege to say Grace before the meal.

The young man prayed long and fervently. He prayed for the sick and the poor. He even prayed for the sinners and the criminals.

Finally when the couple left the house, the girl said to her friend, "Hey, I didn't know you were so religious."

The young man replied, **"I didn't know your father was a Pharmacist!!!"**

Before retiring on his wedding night, the young minister turned to his bride and murmured, "Pardon me, darling, I'm going to pray for guidance."

"Sweetheart," his wife answered, **"I'll take care of your guidance. You pray for endurance!!"**

CHURCH SIGN:
This church is prayer conditioned.

Cures for everything ...

The pastor paid a visit to sweet and innocent Miss Bee, who was in her 80s. She invited him to take a seat in her Victorian parlour while she prepared a little tea. The young minister noticed a cut glass bowl filled with water, sitting on a piano organ. He was shocked to see, of all things, floating in the water, a condom. When she returned with tea and cookies, they began to chat. Finally his curiosity got the better of him. "Miss Bee," he said, pointing to the bowl, "I wonder if you could tell me about this."

"Oh yes," she replied, "Isn't it wonderful? I was walking downtown last fall, and I found this little package. It said to put it on the organ and keep it wet, and it would prevent disease. **And you know, I think it's working! I haven't had a cold all winter!!!**"

Announcements in Hong Kong's church bulletin:

'Thursday at 5 PM there will be a meeting of the Little Mothers' Club. All those wishing to become little mothers will please meet the minister in the study.'

'The ladies of the church have cast off clothing of every kind, and they can be seen in the church basement on Friday afternoon.'

This being Easter Sunday, we will ask Mrs. Brown to come forward and lay an egg on the altar.

At the Pearly Gates

The Entrance test

Three guys arrived at the Pearly Gates and asked St Peter to admit them to Heaven.

"All right, but first, each of you must answer a simple question correctly." He asked the 1st. "What was the name of the first man God created?"

"Adam" came the reply.

"Correct. Enter." said St Peter.

He asked the 2nd. "What was the name of the first woman God created?"

"Eve," came the reply from the 2nd man.

"Correct. Enter."

The 3rd man was worried and said, "St Peter, would you please make it an easy one for me, too?"

"Okay. Tell me; what were the first few words Eve said when she first saw Adam."

"That's a hard one." said the 3rd man.

"Correct. Enter." said St Peter.

... and Permanent Residence

A man arrived at the Pearly Gates and asked for admission to heaven.

St Peter checked his records and said, "Not possible. You have been married and divorced three times. But wait. On second thought, you may enter."

"Why the sudden change of mind?" asked the man.

"Because," replied St Peter, **"you have gone through hell many times!!"**

The promise
Two Rotarians, Tom and Dick, very close friends, promised each other that whoever died first, would visit earth and tell the other about heaven. It so happened that Tom died and a few years later, he visited Dick.
Dick: "How's heaven, Tom?"
Tom: "Very good, Dick. They even have a Rotary Club here. In fact, they are having a meeting right now."
Dick: "But Tom, why did you leave the meeting to visit me?"
Tom: **"Because I've come to tell you that you are our next speaker!"**

At the Pearly Gates, St Peter invited 3 building contractors to give a quote for repairing the broken stairway to Heaven.
One was from Singapore, one from America and one from India.
The Singapore contractor studied the stairway and quoted $30,000 for the job, saying $10,000 for the materials, $10,000 for the workmanship and $10,000 for overheads and profit.
The American contractor quoted $60,000 saying $20,000 for the materials, $20,000 for workmanship and $20,000 for overheads and profit.
The Indian quoted $90,000 for the same job.
St Peter asked, "Can you give me a breakdown?"
"Sure, St Peter," said the Indian, **"$30,000 for you, $30,000 for me and $ 30,000 for the Singapore guy to do the job."**

Visitors pass ...
A guy arrives at the Pearly Gates and is admitted to Heaven. Eager to know what it is like in Hell, he requests for a visit and his request is granted. When he arrives in Hell, a huge white chauffeur-driven Rolls Royce comes to receive him. He is taken sightseeing and is shown all the beautiful bars, Karaoke lounges, beaches flooded with beautiful blondes and brunettes. At the end of the tour, he is treated to a King's feast in a palace. The guy returns to Heaven very much impressed, and appeals to St. Peter to transfer him to Hell instead. His request is granted. Upon his arrival, he is immediately taken away by the Demons and severely tortured. "Why?" he protests, "What happened to all the luxuries and pleasures I witnessed before."
Demon: **"The last time you visited you were a Tourist. Now you're an Immigrant!!"**

The children were lined up in the cafeteria of a Catholic elementary school for lunch. At the head of the table was a large pile of apples.
The nun made a note, and posted on the apple tray: **"Take only ONE. God is watching."**
Moving further along the lunch line, at the other end of the table was a large pile of chocolate chip cookies.
A child had written a note**, "Take all you want. God is watching the apples."**

At the Bar

Getting to know you ...
A cowboy - dressed to kill with cowboy shirt, hat, jeans, spurs and chaps - went to a bar and ordered a drink. As he sat there sipping his whiskey, a young lady sat down next to him. After she ordered her drink, she turned to the cowboy.
Lady: "Are you a real cowboy?"
Cowboy: "Well, I've spent my whole life on the ranch, herding cows, breaking horses, mending fences, so I guess I am. What do you do?"
Lady: "I'm a lesbian. I spend my whole day thinking about women. I get up in the morning thinking of women, when I eat, shower, watch TV - everything makes me think of women."
After she left, a couple sat down next to the cowboy.
Couple: "Are you a real cowboy?"
Cowboy: "I always thought I was, but **I just found out that I'm a lesbian!!**"

❖

The ol' ball and chain
Bartender: "I think you've had enough, sir."
Drunk: "I just lost my wife, buddy."
Bartender: Well, it must be hard losing a wife...
Drunk: "It was almost impossible!!"

❖

It's on the house
A guy runs into a bar, totally out of breath. "Give me ten double whiskeys," panted the guy. As soon as he was served, he proceeded to gulp down the drinks one by one.
"You look like hell," said the barman. "Why are you drinking so fast?"
"You'd be drinking this fast, if you had what I had." said the guy.
"Oh, geez, I'm sorry," the barman said apologetically. "What have you got?"
The guy looked at him and said, **"Two dollars!!"**

Getting sober ...
A man walked into a bar and ordered three Gin and Tonics. He came every week and got the same until one day the bartender asked why he always ordered three drinks and the man answered, "When I left Mexico my two brothers told me to have a drink for them."
A few weeks later the man only ordered two drinks and the bartender asked, "If you don't mind my asking, did something happen to one of your brothers?"
"No" said the man, **"I quit drinking!!"**

"Please, bartender, put two cherries in my Manhattan. **My doctor told me to eat more fruit.**

School – the best years of our life ...

The chatterbox

Eight-year-old Sally brought her report card home from school. Her marks were good...mostly A's and a couple of B's. However, her teacher had written across the bottom: "Sally is a smart little girl, but she has one fault. She talks too much in school. I have an idea which I think may break her of the habit."

Sally's dad signed her report card, putting a note on the back: **"Please let me know if your idea works on Sally because I would like to try it out on her mother!"**

So well-versed ...

A pretty young schoolteacher concerned about one of her 11-year-old students, took him aside after class one day.

Teacher: "Victor, why has your schoolwork been so poor lately?"

Victor: "I can't concentrate, I've fallen in love."

Teacher: "Is that so? And with whom?"

Victor: "With you,"

Teacher: "But Victor, don't you see how silly that is? It's true that I would like a husband of my own someday. But I don't want a child."

Victor: "Oh, don't worry. I'll be careful!"

Solve the mystery

The visiting church school supervisor asked little Johnny during Bible class, "Who broke down the walls of Jericho."

Little Johnny replied that he did not know, but it definitely was not him.

The supervisor, taken aback by this lack of basic Bible knowledge went to the school principal and related the whole incident. The principal replied that he knew little Johnny and his whole family very well and could vouch for them. If little Johnny said that he did not do it, he believed that he was telling the truth.

Even more appalled, the inspector went to the regional Head of Education and related the whole story. After listening the Head replied: "I can't see why you are making such a big issue out of this; **just get three quotes and fix the damned wall.**"

First day at school

Little Johnny came home from his first day of school and said "Mommy, the teacher asked me today if I have any brothers or sisters who will be coming to school."

"That's nice of her to take such an interest, dear. What did she say when you told her you are the only child?"

She just said, **"Thank goodness!"**

A whale of a tale
A little girl was talking to her teacher about whales. The teacher said it was physically impossible for a whale to swallow a human because even though it is a very large mammal its throat is very small.
The little girl then stated that a whale swallowed Jonah.
Irritated, the teacher reiterated that a whale could not swallow a human; it was physically impossible.
The little girl said, "When I get to heaven I will ask Jonah".
The teacher asked, "What if Jonah went to hell?"
The little girl replied, **"Then you ask him!"**

Fair exchange ...
A professor handed out the test papers to all of his students and returned to his desk to wait.
When the test was over, the students handed their papers in. As the professor was going through the papers, he noticed one student had paper-clipped a $100 bill to his test with an accompanying note saying **"A buck a point"**
The next day the professor handed the tests back to the respective students.
The student who attached the $100 bill to his, received his test score back along with $64 and a note saying, **"Here's your change!"**

The school teacher was angry with the doctor's son.
"I will certainly have to ask your father to come and see me," she remarked.
"You'd better not," said the boy, **"he charges $200 a visit."**

A Sunday school teacher asked the children just before she dismissed them to go to church, "And why is it necessary to be quiet in church?"
Annie replied, **"Because people are sleeping."**

The spirit of the thing ...
A professor of chemistry wanted to teach his 5th grade class a lesson about the evils of liquor, so he produced an experiment that involved a glass of water, a glass of whiskey, and two worms.
"Now, class, observe what happens to each worm," said the professor, putting one worm into the water.
The worm in the water writhed about happily.
He put the second worm, into the whiskey. It writhed painfully, and quickly sank to the bottom, dead as a doornail.
"Now, what lesson can we derive from this experiment?" the professor asked.
Little Johnny raised his hand and wisely responded;
"Drink whiskey and you won't get worms!"

❖

What you learn at finishing school ...

Q: What do you do if your boyfriend walks out?
A: Close the door!

❖

Q: When do you care for a man's company?
A: When he owns it!

❖

Q: What did God say after creating man?
A: I must be able to do better than that!

❖

Q: Why do men buy electric lawnmowers?
A: So they can find their way back to the house!

❖

Q: What is the one thing that all men at singles bars have in common?
A: They're married!

❖

If vegetarians eat vegetables, what do humanitarians eat?!

❖

Keeping company ...
A new teacher was trying to make use of her psychology courses. She started her class by saying, "Everyone who thinks he is stupid, stand up!"
After a few seconds, little Johnny stood up. The teacher was surprised, but realized this was an opportune moment to help a child.
"Do you think you're stupid, Johnny?" she asked.
"No, ma'am," Johnny replied, **"but I hate to see you standing there all by yourself!"**

The punishment
Miss Fig Pot was found guilty in a traffic court and when asked for her occupation she said, "I'm a school teacher."
The judge rose from the bench, smiled with delight, and said. "I have waited years for a schoolteacher to appear before this court. **Now sit down at that table and write 'I will not run a red light' five hundred times."**

Teacher: "Cindy, why are you doing your math multiplication on the floor?"
Cindy: "You told me to do it **without using tables!"**

105

Jesus can't drive ...
A Sunday school teacher of preschoolers asked the students to learn one fact about Jesus by the following Sunday. The following week she asked each child in turn what he or she had learned.

Susie said, "He was born in a manger."

Bobby said, "He threw the money changers out of the temple."

Little Johnny said, "He has a red pickup truck but he doesn't know how to drive it."

Curious, the teacher asked, "And where did you learn that, Johnny?"

"From my Daddy," said Johnny. "Yesterday we were driving down the highway, and this red pickup truck pulled out in front of us and Daddy yelled at him, **'Jesus Christ! Why don't you learn how to drive?'** "

Making the grade
Little Johnny wasn't getting good marks in school. One day he surprised the teacher with an announcement.

He tapped her on the shoulder and said, "I don't want to scare you, but my daddy says if I don't get better grades... **somebody is going to get a spanking!"**

Hard work never killed anybody. But why take the risk.

Animals and Such

For Love or Money

Once there was a millionaire, who collected live alligators. He kept them in the pool at the back of his mansion. He also had a beautiful daughter. During a party he gave one day, he announced, "I will give one million dollars, or my daughter, to the man who can swim across this pool full of alligators and emerge unharmed!"

As soon as he finished his last word, there was the sound of a large splash in the pool. The guy in the pool was swimming with all his might and the crowd began to cheer him on.

Finally, he made it to the other side unharmed.

The millionaire was impressed. He said, "That was incredible! Fantastic! Well, I must keep my end of the bargain. Do you want my daughter or the one million dollars?"

The guy caught his breath, and then said, "Listen, I don't want your money! And I don't want your daughter! **I just want the guy who pushed me into the pool !!**"

Wife: "We've got such a clever dog. He brings in the daily newspapers every morning."
Husband: "Well lots of dogs can do that."
Wife: "But we've never subscribed to any newspapers!!"

Survivor ...
Two men are being chased by a bear, which is rapidly gaining on them. The first man stops to put on some running shoes.
"I don't know why you're bothering," screams the second "we can't outrun a grizzly!"
"I don't need to outrun him," returns the first, **"all I've got to do is outrun you!"**

Out bid
One day a man went to an auction. He saw a parrot he really wanted and began to bid for it. He got caught up in the bidding and kept on making offers. Finally, after he bid much more than he intended, he won the bid - the parrot was his at last!
Man: "I sure hope this parrot can talk. I would hate to have paid this much for it, only to find out that he can't talk!"
Auctioneer: **"Don't worry. He can talk. Who do you think kept bidding against you?"**

What are a woman's four favourite animals?
A **mink** in the closet, a **Jaguar** in the garage, a **tiger** in her bedroom and a **donkey** to pay for it all.

Airlines ...

The friendly handshake ...
It was past midnight on the SIA flight, and all the lights were off. A little boy nudged his sleeping mother and said, "Mom, can I go by myself to pee?"
"Okay," replied the sleepy mother, "but be sure to shake it twice after you have finished."
Later, the worried Mother went to help lest he forgot to shake. She put her hand inside the door and shook it twice. Returning to her seat, she was shocked to see her son in deep sleep. As she was recovering from the shock, she overheard a passenger coming out from the same bathroom saying, **"What a fantastic service. I have yet to see a service that tops that!!!!!!"**

Attention please ...
Announcement on a public transportation vehicle while in Orlando.
"When you exit this vehicle, please be sure to lower your head and watch your step. If you fail to do so, please lower your voice and watch your language. Thank you."

Opportunist: A person who starts taking a bath if he falls into a river

Sex or Alcohol ...
On an airline flight, a guy was seated next to an elderly priest. A minor technical problem at the gate delayed the flight, so the captain announced that the airline would be offering a free round of drinks as an apology.

When the charming and attractive flight attendant came by, the guy ordered a double scotch. He leaned back with his drink as the attendant asked the priest if he would like a drink.

"Oh, no thank you," replied the priest. "I would rather commit adultery than drink alcohol."

Choking on his swallow of scotch, the guy quickly put his drink back on the beverage cart. **"Excuse me, miss, I didn't know I had a choice!!"**

Losing your cool
Shortly after take off from Kennedy airport, the captain made an announcement over the intercom, "Ladies and Gentlemen, this is your captain speaking. Welcome to Flight 293. The weather ahead is good and we should have a smooth flight, now sit back and relax. **OH MY GOD!**" There was silence. Then, the captain spoke again "Ladies and Gentlemen, I apologise if I scared you earlier, but while I was talking, the flight attendant accidentally spilled hot coffee in my lap. You should see the front of my pants!"

A passenger in the rear seat said: **"That's nothing. He should see the back of mine!!"**

Flying lessons
A photographer for a national magazine was assigned to take pictures of a great forest fire. When he arrived at the airstrip just an hour before sundown, a small Cessna airplane was waiting for him. He jumped in with his equipment and shouted, "Let's go!" The tense man sitting in the pilot's seat swung the plane into the wind and soon they were in the air.
"Fly over the north side of the fire," said the photographer, "and make several low-level passes."
"Why?" asked the nervous pilot?
"Because I'm a photographer, and photographers take pictures!"
After a long pause, the pilot replied: **"You mean, you're not my instructor?"**

"I am" is reportedly the shortest sentence in the English language.
Could it be that **"I do"** is the longest sentence.

A businessman was confused about a bill he had received, so he asked his secretary for some mathematical help. "If I were to give you $20,000, minus 14%, how much would you take off?"
The secretary replied, **"Everything except my earrings."**

A taxing matter

Undercover broker
The stockbroker received notice from the IRS that he was being audited. He showed up at the appointed time and place with all his financial records, and then sat for what seemed like hours as the auditor scrutinized their every detail.

Finally, the IRS agent looked up and commented, "You must have been a tremendous fan of Sir Arthur Conan Doyle."

"Why would you say that?" wondered the broker.

"Because you've made more brilliant deductions on your last three returns than Sherlock Holmes made in his entire career!"

Now I lay me down to sleep ...
A couple of weeks after hearing a sermon on Psalms 51:2-4 (knowing my own hidden secrets) and Psalms 52: 3-4(lies and deceit), a man wrote the following letter to the IRS:

"I have been unable to sleep, knowing that I have cheated on my income tax. I understated my taxable income and have enclosed a cheque for $150.
Sincerely,
Taxpayer
P.S. If I still can't sleep, I will send the rest!!

Computer Savvy

Compaq is considering changing the command 'Press Any Key' to 'Press Return Key' because of the flood of calls asking where the **'Any'** key is.

A Dell customer called to say he couldn't get his computer to fax anything. After 40 minutes of trouble-shooting, the technician discovered the man was trying to fax a piece of paper by holding it in front of the monitor screen and hitting the **'Send'** key.

A confused caller to IBM was having trouble printing documents. He told the technician that the computer had said it 'couldn't find printer'. The user had also tried turning the computer screen to face the printer; however, his computer still couldn't **'see'** the printer.

A woman called the Canon helpdesk because her printer refused to print. The tech asked her if she was running it under Windows. The woman responded, "No, my desk is next to the door. The man sitting in the cubicle next to me is under a window and his printer is working fine."

Lawyers and Judges

The gentle cricketers ...
Judge: "Little girl, now that your parents are getting divorced, do you want to live with your Mummy?"
Child: "No, my Mummy beats me."
Judge: "Well then, I guess you want to live with your Daddy."
Child: "No, my Daddy beats me too."
Judge: "Well then, who do you want to live with?"
Child: "I want to live with the Indian Cricket team, they never beat anybody!!!"

A judicial gathering ...
A man passed on and found himself in heaven. Unhappy with his accommodation, he complained to St. Peter. He was told he would have to wait at least three years before his appeal could be heard.
The guy protested but his words fell on deaf ears.
He was then approached by the devil who told him that he could arrange for an appeal to be heard in a few days. In exchange, the man would have to be willing to change the venue to Hell.
When the guy asked why appeals could be heard so much sooner in Hell, he was told, **"We have all the lawyers and judges here!!!"**

It's all about the money
A very successful lawyer parked his brand-new Lexus in front of the office. As he opened the door, a truck came along, and completely tore off the driver's door! The attorney immediately grabbed his cell phone, hit speed dial for 911, and had a policeman there in three minutes.

Before the cop had a chance to ask any questions, the lawyer started screaming hysterically. His brand new Lexus would never be the same, no matter how well the car was repaired.

When the lawyer finally stopped ranting, the cop shook his head in disgust and disbelief.

"You lawyers are so materialistic that you don't notice anything else."

"How can you say such a thing?" the lawyer responded indignantly.

The cop replied, "You didn't even notice that your left arm is missing from the elbow down! It must have been torn off when the truck hit you."

"OH, NO!" screamed the lawyer in shock. **"Where is my Rolex???"**

Did you know...
Do you know how many lawyer jokes there really are in the world? **Only three.** The rest are true stories.

If you can't get a lawyer who knows the law, get one who knows the judge.

Mr. Scrooge

A local charity office sent a rep to the town's most successful lawyer who had never made a contribution. "Our research shows that out of a yearly income of at least $500,000, you don't give a penny to charity. Wouldn't you like to give back to the community in some way?"

The lawyer mulled over this for a moment and replied, "First, did your research also show that my mother is dying after a long illness and has medical bills that are several times her annual income?"

Embarrassed, the rep mumbled, "Um...no."

"--Or that my brother is blind and confined to a wheelchair?"

The stricken rep began to stammer an apology as the lawyer's voice rose in indignation,

"--Or that my sister's husband died, leaving her penniless with three children!"

"I had no idea..." replied the stricken rep only to be cut off once again by the lawyer, **"--And if I don't give them a penny, why should I give any to you?!!"**

A Guy called a plumber to the house to fix a leak. The plumber completed the job in 15 minutes and asked for his fee of $50.00 for the service.

"What!" shouted the customer, "I don't even charge that much for my legal consultation."

"Yes, I know," replied the plumber, **"That's why I quit being a lawyer!"**

Getting the facts
A lawyer was questioning a witness to an automobile accident.
Lawyer: "Did you actually see the accident?"
Witness: "Yes, sir."
Lawyer: "How far away were you when the accident happened?"
Witness: "Thirty-one feet, six and one quarter inches."
Lawyer (thinking he'd trap the witness): "Well, sir, will you tell the jury how you knew it was exactly that distance?"
Witness: "Because when the accident happened I took out a tape and measured it. **I knew some stupid lawyer would ask me that question!**"

Two of a kind ...
3 guys were in a boat that was about to sink. They saw a small island not too far away.
The businessman jumped into the water and started swimming towards the island. But before he could reach it the sharks attacked him.
The Doctor has also jumped into the water and the sharks attacked him too.
The third guy, a lawyer also jumped and reached the island safely.
The people on the island asked him, "Why didn't the sharks attack you."
The lawyer replied, **"Professional courtesy!"**

Cold-blooded linguists
Someone mistakenly leaves the cages open in the reptile house at the Bronx Zoo and there are snakes slithering all over the place. Frantically, the keeper tries everything, but he can't get them back in their cages. Finally he says, "Quick, call a lawyer!"
"A lawyer? Why??"
"We need someone who speaks their language!!"

The heart of the matter ...
A guy with a damaged heart visited a Heart Surgeon for a heart transplant.
The surgeon said, "In this freezer I have a heart of a businessman. He drank, smoked, and gambled – all in moderation. It will cost you $20,000.00.
If you want better, then I have the heart of a Rotarian. He drank a little but never smoked or gambled. It will cost you $50,000.00.
And if you are looking for the best," continued the surgeon, "then I have a heart of a man who drank, smoked and gambled **heavily**. It will cost you $100,000.00."
"Why so high for this one, Doc.?" Asked the guy.
"Well," explained the surgeon, "this heart belongs to a **solicitor and it has never been used**
The guy thought for a while and chose the heart of the solicitor. After the successful transplant, the guy got his $100,000.00 back. **He sued the Doctor for malpractice.**

Are blondes really dumb...?

Read the instructions
One day, a wife, a blonde, decides to show her husband that blondes really are smart.

When her husband leaves for work the next day, she decides to paint a couple of rooms in the house.

In the evening her husband returns home to the strong smell of paint. He walks into the living room and finds his wife lying on the floor in a pool of sweat clad in a ski jacket and a fur coat. He asks what she is doing. She replies that she wants to prove to him that not all blonde women are dumb and that she has intelligently painted the rooms. He then asks her why she has a ski jacket over her fur coat.

Her reply: "The instructions on the paint can said ...
For best results, put on two coats!!!

The blonde walks into work with her newly bought thermos flask.

Her boss asks, "What is that shiny object with you?"

She said, "It's a special flask, boss?"

The boss then asks, "What does it do?"

She replies, "It keeps hot things hot and cold things cold."

The boss said, "Wow, what do you have in it?"

The blonde replies, "Two cups of **coffee and a coke**."

At the bus stop

Two blondes are waiting at a bus stop, when a bus pulls up and the door opens. One of the blondes leans inside and asks the driver: "Will this bus take me to 5th Avenue?"

The bus driver shakes his head and says, "No, I'm sorry."

Hearing this, the other blonde leans inside, smiles and twitters**, "Will it take ME?"**

Tips on how to answer multiple-choice questions

The blonde reports for her University final examination, which consists of **"yes/no"** type questions. She takes her seat in the examination hall, stares at the question paper for five minutes, and then in a fit of inspiration takes her purse out, removes a coin and starts tossing the coin and marking the answer sheet - **Yes for Heads and No for Tails.**

Within half an hour, she is all done whereas the rest of the class is sweating it out. During the last few minutes, she is seen desperately throwing the coin, swearing and sweating.

Moderator: "Is anything the matter?"

Blonde: **"I finished the exam in half and hour. But, I am rechecking my answers."**

Road rules
Two blond guys are driving a car on a very hilly road. They get to the top of a very high, steep hill and they start going down it very fast.
The guy driving says "Oh my god! The brakes don't work!"
 "Don't worry," said the guy in the passenger seat, "**there's a stop sign at the end of this hill!!"**

❖

A weighty business ...
A blonde holding a baby walks into a drug store and asks the clerk if she can use the store's baby scale.
"Sorry, ma'am," says the clerk. "Our baby scale is broken. But we can figure out the baby's weight if we weigh mother and baby together on the adult scale, and then weigh the mother alone, and then subtract the second number from the first."
"Oh, that won't work," says the blonde."
Why not?" asks the clerk
"Because," she answers, "I'm not the mother, I'm the aunt!!!"

❖

What's your hobby ...
A highway patrolman pulled alongside a speeding car on the freeway.
Glancing at the car, he was astounded to see that the blonde behind the wheel was knitting! The trooper cranked down his window and yelled to the driver, **"PULL OVER!"**
"NO," the blonde yelled back, "It's a Scarf!!"

❖

Why Gentlemen prefer blondes
A beautiful and hopeful blonde applied to Medical School; needless to say, she never made it. These are some of the answers she gave at the entrance exam:

SEMEN – sailors

ARTERY – the study of fine paintings

BOWEL – letters like a, e, i, o, u

CARDIOLOGY – advanced study of poker playing

GENES – blue denim

COMA – punctuation mark

IMPOTENT – distinguished, well-known

GROIN – to mash to a pulp / smile

HYMEN – greeting to several males

OBESITY – city of Obe

ULTRASOUND – radical noise

SECRETION – hiding anything

TUMOR – extra pair

❖

Country bumpkins

Be thankful to God
After losing his donkey a yokel got down on his knees and started thanking God.
A passer-by saw him and asked, "Your donkey is missing; what are you thanking God for?"
The yokel replied "I am thanking Him because I wasn't riding the donkey at that time, **otherwise I would have been missing too!**"

Muldoon wanted to sell his old battered Suzuki car, which had done more than 100,000km. Since nobody was inclined to buy it, he approached his friend to help him sell it off. The friend advised him to have the mileage meter reading reduced to around 30,000 km so that he could tell the prospective customer that it has been used sparingly. Muldoon liked the idea.
A few weeks later, the same friend met him and enquired whether he was able to dispose of his car.
Muldoon replied, "Are you mad? **Who sells a car which has done only 30,000km!!**"

Why did Blanco take 17 of his friends to a movie?
Because the poster said, **"Below 18 not allowed".**

Blanco: (Buying a TV) "Do you have colour TVs?"
Salesman: "Sure."
Blanco: "Give me a green one, please!"

❖

Blanco calls Air India. "How long does it take to fly to Delhi?"
Rep: "Just a minute,"
Blanco: "Thank you." and hangs up.

❖

Why can't morons make ice cubes?
They always forget the recipe.

❖

What will a moron do after making photocopies?
He will compare it with the original for **spelling mistakes!!**

❖

What will a moron do if he wants an additional white sheet of paper?
He takes a photocopy of the white paper!!

❖

Job-hunter
Blanco was filling up an application form for a job. He filled the columns titled NAME, AGE, and ADDRESS etc. Then he came to the column "Salary Expected":
After much thought he wrote: Yes!!

Croc in boots ...
Muldoon proposes to a woman.
She says, "Yes I'll marry you, if you bring me a pair of crocodile boots."
Muldoon immediately sets off to Africa and disappears. Finally, a search is made; they find him hunting crocodiles and watch him killing a huge one. Muldoon walks over to the reptile, checks its legs and angrily exclaims **"71 crocs and still no boots!"**

The doctor told Blanco, who was over-weight, that if he ran eight kilometres a day for 300 days, he would loose 34 kilos.
At the end of 300 days, Blanco called the doctor to report he had lost weight, but he had a problem.
"What's the problem?" asked the doctor.
"I'm 2,400km from home!!"

Budget travel to heaven

Blanco holding an economy class ticket boarded the Air India flight for Delhi and took a seat in First class. Despite requests to take his seat in Economy class, he would not budge. Finally, another passenger sitting in First class came to help. He whispered something to Blanco. Blanco immediately expressed gratitude and quietly walked to his seat in Economy class.

Stunned by the scene, the crew thanked the passenger and asked, "Sir, we are curious to know how you handled this stubborn passenger."

"Simple, I just told him that the back compartment goes to Delhi and this compartment goes to Russia!!

The punishment ...

Blanco was chatting with his friend.

Blanco: One day I came home and found my wife making love with our chauffeur, on the sofa.

Friend: "That's bad, did you sack the chauffeur?"

Blanco: "No, but I did something more severe."

Friend: "I hope you did not divorce your wife."

Blanco: "No, I did something more drastic."

Friend: "Oh, my God, don't tell me you killed her?"

Blanco: "No, I did something even more drastic.
 I sold the sofa!!"

Replacement stud

A farmer's daughter answers the door and sees an older neighbour there.

Girl: "My father isn't home, but I know what you want and I can help you. My father charges $100 for his best bull to service your cow."

Neighbour: "That's not what I want."

Girl: "We have a young bull who is just starting out. My father charges $50 for him."

Neighbour: "That's not what I want."

Girl: "We have an old bull out in the pasture. He can still do the job. My father charges only ten dollars for him."

Neighbour: "That's not what I want. I came here to see your father about your brother, Elmer. He made my daughter pregnant."

Girl: "Oh. You'll have to see my father about that because **I don't know what he charges for Elmer!!**"

Why can't a moron dial 911?
He cannot find eleven on the phone!

How do you make a moron laugh on Saturday?
Tell him a joke on Wednesday.

Politically correct

Dear God ...
A little boy wanted $100 badly and prayed hard for two weeks but nothing happened. Then he decided to write GOD a letter asking for the $100.

When the postal authorities received the letter **GOD USA,** they decided to send it to President Bush.

The President was so impressed, touched, and amused that he instructed his secretary to send the little boy a five-dollar bill. President Bush thought this would appear to be a lot of money to a little boy.

The little boy was delighted with the five dollars and sat down to write a thank you note to GOD, which read:

"Dear GOD, Thank you very much for sending the money, however, I noticed that for some reason you had to send it through Washington D.C. and, **as usual, according to Daddy, those rascals deducted $95.00!!"**

Late one night, a mugger wearing a ski mask jumped into the path of a well-dressed man and stuck a gun in his ribs. "Give me your money," he demanded.

Indignant, the affluent man replied, "You can't do this, I'm a United States Congressman!"

"In that case," replied the mugger, **"give me MY money!"**

Dirty politics ...
One day a cannibal visited the neighbouring island of cannibals. There he found that people were being sold at $2 and the politicians at $25.

The visiting cannibal asked, "Why do politicians cost so much?"

The chief answered, **"Do you know how hard it is to clean one of those?!"**

It doesn't pay to lie ...
A busload of politicians was driving down a country road when, all of a sudden, the bus ran off the road and crashed into a tree in an old farmer's field.

The old farmer, after seeing what happened, went over to investigate. He then proceeded to dig a hole and bury the politicians.

A few days later, the local sheriff came out, saw the crashed bus and asked the old farmer where all the politicians had gone.

The old farmer said he had buried them.

The sheriff asked the old farmer, "Were they ALL dead?"

The old farmer replied, **"Well, some of them said they weren't, but you know how those politicians lie!!"**

Politician: One who **shakes** your hand before elections and your Confidence after.

Democracy as we know it ...

American Democracy: The government promises to give you two cows if you vote for it. After the election, the president is impeached for speculating in cow futures. The press dubs the affair "Cow gate".
The cow sues you for breach of contract.

British Democracy: You have two cows. You feed them sheep's brains and they go mad.
The government doesn't do anything.

Representative Democracy: You have two cows. Your neighbours pick someone to tell you who gets the milk.

Pure Democracy: You have two cows.
Your neighbours decide who gets the milk.

Singaporean Democracy: You have two cows.
The Government fines you for keeping two unlicensed farm animals in an HDB apartment.

EUROPEAN DEMOCRACY: You have two cows. At first the government regulates what you can feed them and when you can milk them. Then it pays you not to milk them. After that it takes both, shoots one, milks the other and pours the milk down the drain. Then it requires you to fill out forms accounting for the missing cows.

Golf - all in the game

Lawn delivery ...
A golfer rushed his wife to the hospital for delivery of the baby but didn't quite make it. So the baby was delivered on the front lawn of the hospital.
When the golfer got the bill it showed item No.3 as **-**
'$150.00 for Use of Delivery Room'
The golfer sent a protest letter saying, "The Baby was born on the lawn and not in the Delivery Room."
The Hospital administrator read the letter, and issued a new bill showing alteration on item No.3 as –
'Greens Fee $150.00'!

Golfer: "I'd move heaven and earth to break 100 on this course."
Caddy: "Try heaven, you've already moved most of the earth!!"

Golfer: "Do you think my game is improving?"
Caddy: "Yes sir, you miss the ball much closer now!"

Golfer: "Do you think it's a sin to play on Sunday?"
Caddy: "The way you play, sir, it's a sin on any day!"

Spoken like a true Scotsman
A Scotsman wanting to play golf visited a golf club and hired a third class caddie.
He asked the caddie, "Are you good at finding balls?"
"Yes sir," replied the caddie, "I am very good at finding balls."
"Good" said the Scotsman **"find one and let's get started!!"**

❖

Golfer: "Do you think I can get there with a 5 iron?"
Caddy: "Eventually!"

❖

Golfer: "You've got to be the worst caddy in the world."
Caddy: "I don't think so sir. That would be too much of a coincidence!"

❖

They say, "In life, there are two things a Golfer should never change. One is a golf putter and the other is a wife."
The only difference is, in the case of a putter, **you can try others!!"**

❖

Two men are talking to each other.
1ˢᵗ man: My doctor says I can't play golf.
2ⁿᵈ man: Did he examine you?
1ˢᵗ man: **No, he played with me.**

❖

Golfer: "This is the worst course I've ever played on."
Caddy: "This isn't the golf course. We left that an hour ago!"

"You really shouldn't be playing off the ladies tee."
"I am not. I've duffed three times."

Golfer: "Please stop checking your watch all the time. It's too much of a distraction."
Caddy: "Sir, it's not a watch. It's a compass!!"

Riddle - Why do golfers carry an extra pair of pants?
Answer - Because they might get a hole in one!

❖

One day a golfer opened his wife's secret drawer and found 8 golf balls & $2000 cash. Curious, he asked his wife to explain.
"Well," she confessed," every time I was unfaithful to you I put in a golf ball in the drawer."
"Okay dear, I too have been 8 times unfaithful to you. We are now even. But tell me what's secret about cash?"
"Well dear," she replied, "Every time I accumulated a dozen balls, **I cashed them at the Pro – shop.**

Doctors and Patients

The workers cure for constipation
A production worker goes to the doctor and says, "Doc, I'm constipated."
The doctor examines him for a minute and then says, "Lean over the table."
The construction worker leans over the table, the doctor whacks him on the ass with a baseball bat, CRACK…and then sends him into the bathroom.
He comes out a few minutes later and says, "Doc, I feel great. What should I do to prevent constipation?"
The doctor says, **"Stop wiping with cement bags!"**

Doctor am I sick yet?
It's just a cold," the doctor said. "There is no cure, and you'll just have to live with it until it goes away.
"But Doctor," the patient whined, "it's making me so miserable."
The doctor rolled his eyes toward the ceiling. Then he said, "Look, go home and take a hot bath. Then put a bathing suit on and run around the block three or four times."
"What!" the patient exclaimed. "I'll get pneumonia!"
"We have a cure for pneumonia!!" the doctor said.

Most doctors are good. They will not operate unless they really need the money.

Peeping Tom

A woman went to her psychiatrist because she was having severe problems with her sex life. Unable to get a clear picture of her problems, he asked, "Do you ever watch your husband's face while you are having sex?"

The woman says, "Well, yes, I did once."

"Well, how did he look?" asks the doctor

"Very angry" says the woman.

At this point, the psychiatrist felt that he was really getting somewhere and he said, "How did you see his face that time?"

"He was looking through the window at me!"

What did you eat?

Patient: "Doc, I have noted that you always ask your patients what they eat for dinner."

"Yes," replied the Doctor, **"it gives me an indication how to bill them."**

All night therapy

The woman seated herself in the psychiatrist's office. "What seems to be the problem?" the doctor asked.

"Well, I, uh," she stammered. "I think I, uh, might be a nymphomaniac."

"I see," he said. "I can help you, but I must advise you that my fee is $80 an hour."

"That's not bad," she replied. **"How much for all night??"**

Famous artist
An artist asked the gallery owner if there had been any interest in his paintings on display at that time.
"I have good news and bad news," the owner replied. "The good news is that a gentleman enquired about your work and wondered if it would appreciate in value after your death. When I told him it would, he bought all 15 of your paintings."
"That's wonderful!" the artist exclaimed. "What's the bad news?"
"The guy was your doctor!!"

How to live to be 100
A man asked his doctor if he thought he'd live to be a hundred.
The doctor asked the man, "Do you smoke or drink?"
"No," he replied," I've never done either."
"Do you gamble, drive fast cars, and fool around with women?" inquired the doctor.
"No, I've never done any of those things either."
"Well then," said the doctor, **"what do you want to live to be a hundred for!!?"**

A psychiatrist is a person who will give you expensive answers that your wife will give you for free.

Graphic imagination

A man goes to a psychiatrist, and tells him, "Doc, I think I have an obsession with sex."

The doctor agrees to examine him and begins by showing him various drawings.

First, the doctor draws a square and asks the man to identify it.

The man immediately says, "Omigosh! Four people having sex! "

Next, the doctor draws a circle, at which the man gasps, and says, "One man having sex."

"Next, the doctor draws a triangle, which, of course, the patient identifies as, "Two women and one man having sex."

The doctor put the drawings away and says to the patient, "Yes, I do believe that you have an obsession with sex."

To which the man replies, "Me? **You're the one drawing all the dirty pictures!"**

Please scream like it hurts

Dentist to Patient: "Would you help me? Could you give out a few of your loudest, most painful screams?"

Patient: "Why, Doc? It wasn't all that bad really"

Dentist: "There are so many people in the waiting room right now and **I don't want to miss my five o'clock tee off time!!"**

Sex drive

"You're in remarkable shape for a man your age," said the doctor to the ninety-year old man after the examination.

"I know it," said the old gentleman. "I've really got only one complaint - my sex drive is too high. Got anything you can do for that, Doc?"

The doctor's mouth dropped open. "Your what?" he gasped.

"My sex drive," said the old man. "It's too high, and I'd like to have you lower it if you can."

"Lower it?" exclaimed the doctor, still unable to believe what the ninety-year old gentleman was saying. "Just what do you consider high?"

"These days it seems like it's all in my head, Doc," said the old man, **"and I'd like to have you lower it a couple of feet if you can!!"**

What really goes on in the examination room!

An attractive young girl, chaperoned by an ugly old woman, entered the doctor's office.

"We have come for an examination," said the young girl.

"All right," said the doctor. "Go behind that curtain and take your clothes off."

"No, not me" said the girl. "It's my aunt here."

"Very well," said the doctor. **"Madam, stick out your tongue!!"**

A picture says a thousand words ...
"Do you remember that terribly pushy woman with the attitude problem who lived in the apartment above us?"
"Yes, what about her?"
"She's marrying a doctor she met when she went in for X-rays."
"Really...**I wonder what he saw in her!!**"

Flavour of the day ...
Mrs. Brown was waiting in the doctor's office to get the result of her urine test.
The doctor came out from the Lab and said, "Madam, this bottle you brought in does not contain urine. It's apple juice."
"Oh, my God!" exclaimed Mrs. Brown **"I must have packed the other bottle in my husband's lunch box!!"**

Designer baby ...
A Chinese woman consulted an American gynaecologist. "I can't bear a child. Can you help?"
"Alright," said the gynaecologist, "Just go behind the screen, take off your clothes and I'll be right there."
The woman did not move. The doctor reminded her to go behind the screen and wait for him.
"But Doctor," said the Chinese woman, **"I want a Chinese baby!!"**

A newspaper reporter was interviewing a man on his ninety-ninth birthday. At the end of the interview, the reporter said, "I hope I can come back to see you next year for your hundredth birthday."
To which the old man replied, **"I don't see why not. You look healthy enough!!"**

Wives, can't leave em, can't loose em
The doctor was advising his patient who complained of nervousness.
"Next time," suggested the doctor, "don't take your trouble to bed."
"But Doctor," he replied, **"my wife won't sleep alone."**

Wrong wife
A worried husband phoned the doctor at three in the morning.
"Doctor, please rush to my house. My wife has appendicitis."
"Impossible," said the Doctor, "just give her some carbonated soda and she'll go sleep."
"But doc, it's serious, please come right away"
"Look" said the Doctor, "three years ago I operated on her for appendicitis. Have you ever heard of a 2nd appendix?"
"Doc, ever heard of a 2nd wife!!"

The collector
Patient: "Doctor, my wife thinks I'm crazy because I like sausages."
Psychiatrist: "Nonsense! I like sausages too."
Patient: "Good, you should come see my collection. I've got hundreds of 'em!!"

Then there was this doctor who tried his hand at being a bank robber but failed because the teller couldn't read his handwriting on the hold-up note.

Patient: Doctor, the pills you gave me has made me constipated.
Doctor: How about the ones I gave you earlier?
Patient: Those pills gave me diarrhoea.
Doctor: Hmm…..maybe you should take one of each.

"Doc!" the man yells, "I've lost my memory!"
"Calm down, sir. When did this happen?"
The man looked at him. **"When did what happen?"**

The doctor placed a stethoscope on the woman's chest and said, "Now big breaths."
"Thank you Doc," said the woman, **"and they are real you know."**

Two is better than one
Patient: "Doctor that rectal examination hurt like hell. What did you do?"
Doctor: "I used two fingers."
Patient: "What for?"
Doctor: "I needed a second opinion!"

The referral
A patient was waiting nervously in the examination room of a famous specialist
Specialist: "So **who** did you see before coming to me?"
Patient: "My local General Practitioner."
Specialist: "Your GP? What a waste of time. Tell me, what sort of useless advice did he give you?"
Patient: "He told me to come and see you!!"

Please confirm
Peter called his doctor's office for an appointment. "I'm sorry," said the receptionist, "we can't fit you in for at least two weeks."
"But I could be dead by then!"
"No problem. **If your wife lets us know, we'll cancel the appointment!!"**

The emergency ...
The tired doctor was awakened by a phone call in the middle of the night.
"Please, you have to come right over," pleaded the distraught young mother. "My child has swallowed a contraceptive."
The physician dressed quickly, but before he could get out the door, the phone rang again.
"You don't have to come over after all," the woman said with a sigh of relief. **"My husband just found another one!!"**

Bad news and really bad news ...
There was this fellow who received a phone call from his doctor.
Doctor: "I have some bad news and some really bad news."
Patient: "Let me have it."
Doctor: "The bad news is that I got your test results back and you have only 24 hours to live."
The man groaned, sobbed desperately. Finally he asked the doctor. "What's the really bad news?"
Doctor: **"I forgot to call you yesterday!"**

Food for thought...
Isn't it a bit unnerving that doctors call what they do **"practice"?**

A fourth hand
The doctor answered the phone and heard the familiar voice of a colleague on the other end of the line.
"We need a fourth for poker," said the friend.
"I'll be right over," whispered the doctor.
As he was putting on his coat, his wife asked, "Is it serious?"
"Oh yes, quite serious," said the doctor gravely, **"in fact, there are three doctors there already!"**

Out voted
A man has his annual physical, and afterward the doctor tells him, "You had a great check-up. Is there anything that you'd like to talk about or ask me?"
"Well," the patient says, "I was thinking about getting a vasectomy."
"That's a pretty big decision. Have you talked it over with your family?" the doctor asks.
"Yes, I have," answers the man.
"Well, what did they have to say about it?" the doctor asks.
The man replies, **"They're in favour, 10 to 2."**

"Doctor, you told me I have a month to live and then you sent me a bill for $1,000! I can't pay that before the end of the month!"
"Okay, you have six months to live."

Face up ... face down ...
A very homely person made an appointment with a psychiatrist. The homely person walked into the doctor's office and said, "Doctor, I'm so depressed and lonely. I don't have any friends, no one will come near me, and everybody laughs at me. Can you help me accept my ugliness?"
"I'm sure I can." the psychiatrist replied. **"Just go over and lie face down on that couch!!"**

One skill only ...
At a big cocktail party, an obstetrician's wife noticed another guest, a big, over sexed blonde, making overtures at her husband. It was a large, informal gathering, so she tried to laugh if off until she saw them disappear into a bedroom together.
At once she rushed into the bedroom, pulled the two apart and screamed, "Look you hussy! **My husband just delivers babies, he doesn't INSTALL them!"**

While giving a physical, the doctor noticed that his patient's shins were covered with dark bruises.
"Tell me," said the doctor, "do you play hockey or soccer?"
"Neither," said the man. **"My wIfe and I play bridge."**

❖

The good Samaritan ...
A doctor and a lawyer in two cars collided on a country road. The lawyer, seeing that the doctor was a little shaken up, helped him from the car and offered him a drink from his hipflask. The doctor accepted and handed the flask back to the lawyer, who closed it and put it away.
"Aren't you going to have a drink yourself?" asked the doctor.
"Sure," replied the attorney, **"after the police leave.**

The will
The patient shook his doctor's hand in gratitude and said, "Since we are the best of friends, I will not insult you by offering payment. But I would like you to know that I have mentioned you in my will."
That is very kind of you," said the doctor emotionally and then added, **"May I see that prescription I just gave you? I'd like to make a little change...."**

Jim: Doc, after the operation, will I be able to play the piano after two weeks?
Doctor: I can't promise the piano but the last time I performed this type of operation the patient was playing the harp in two day.

Can you hear me?

There was an elderly gentleman who had a serious hearing problem for a number of years. So, he went to the doctor who fitted him with a fancy hearing aid. A month later, the elderly gentleman went back to the doctor.

Doctor: "Your hearing is perfect. Your family must be really pleased that you can hear again."

To which the gentleman said, "Oh, I haven't told my family yet. I just sit around and listen to the conversations. **I've changed my will three times!**"

Got milk?

One day a farmer died. His elderly, bedridden widow was very depressed. Her son tried everything he could think of to cheer her up but nothing worked. The doctor suggested that he give her a shot of whiskey mixed with her drink nightly to perk her up. Following this advice, the son gave his mother a shot of whisky and milk every evening and found that his mother slept like a baby and woke up feeling wonderful. This went on and his mother woke every morning feeling more and more cheerful.

When the boy suggested one day that they sell the farm and move closer to the city, his mother said, "Son, you can do anything you want to, but **DON'T SELL THAT COW!**"

Things you don't want to hear during surgery:

Better save that. We'll need it for the autopsy.

Wait a minute; if this is his spleen, then what's that?

Oops! Hey, has anyone ever survived 500ml of this stuff before?

Anyone see where I left that scalpel?

You know there's big money in kidneys. Hey, the guy has two of 'em.

Could you stop that thing from beating? It's throwing my concentration off!

I wish I hadn't forgotten my glasses.

Rats! Page 47 of the manual is missing!

Nurse, did this patient sign the organ donation card?

Don't worry. I think it is sharp enough.

FIRE! FIRE! Everyone get out!

Rats, there go the lights again...

Everybody stand back! I lost my contact lens!

The Viagra syndrome

The Viagra experience
A guy took a Viagra pill and died from a heart attack. When they put him in the coffin, they could not close the lid.
Thus comes the phrase "**Die Hard!!**"

❖

Another **death from Viagra** has been reported.
This guy took 10 pills ... and his wife died.

❖

One stiff drink
Have you tried the new hot beverage, "Viagraccino?"
One cup and you're up all night!!

❖

No need for ironing ...
Then there was this guy who left his Viagra tablet in his shirt pocket when he sent it to the laundry.
Now, his shirt is too stiff to wear!!

❖

Thrill rides
Viagra is now being compared to Disneyland –
a one-hour wait for a 2-minute ride!

❖

Telling signs...

Sign in a Japanese hotel:
"You are invited to take advantage of the chambermaid."

❖

Sign in the lobby of a Moscow hotel opposite a Russian Orthodox monastery:
"You are welcome to visit the cemetery where famous Russian and Soviet composers, artists, and writers are buried daily except Thursday!"

❖

Sign in a Rhodes tailor shop:
"Order your summer suit. Because of the big rush we will execute customers in strict rotation!"

❖

Sign in a Rome laundry:
"Ladies, leave your clothes here and spend the afternoon having a good time."

❖

Sign on the menu of a Swiss restaurant:
"Our wines leave you nothing to hope for"

❖

Signs that say it all ...

Sign at the gynaecologist's clinic:
"Dr. Jones, at your cervix"

❖

Sign in a veterinarian's waiting room:
"Be back in 5 minutes. Sit! Stay!"

❖

On the door of a plastic surgeon's office:
"We can help you pick your nose!"

❖

Sign on a maternity room door:
"Push! Push! Push!"

❖

Sign at an optometrist's office:
"If you don't see what you're looking for, you've come to the right place"

❖

Sign on a plumber's truck:
"We repair what your husband fixed"

❖

More meaningful signs ...

Sign on the trucks of a local plumbing company in NE Pennsylvania:
"Don't sleep with a drip. Call your plumber"

Sign outside a muffler shop:
"No appointment necessary. We hear you coming"

Sign on an electrician's truck:
"Let us remove your shorts"

Advertisement for donkey rides in Thailand:
"Would you like to ride on your own ass?"

Sign in a non-smoking area:
"If we see smoke, we will assume you are on fire and take appropriate action"

Sign in the front yard of a funeral home:
"Drive carefully. We'll wait"

All the nations

Leave it to the Japanese ...
It was the first day of school and a new student, the son of a Japanese businessman, entered the fourth grade.
The teacher greeted the class and said, "Let's begin by reviewing some American history."
Who said, "Give me Liberty, or give me death?"
She saw only a sea of blank faces, except for that of Toshiba, who had his hand up.
"Patrick Henry, 1775," said the boy.
"Now," said the teacher, who said; "Government of the people, by the people, for the people shall not perish from the earth?"
Again, no response except from Toshiba: "Abraham Lincoln, 1863."
The teacher snapped at the class, "You should be ashamed. Toshiba, who is new to our country, knows more about it than you do."
As she turned to write something on the blackboard, she heard a loud whisper: "Damned Japanese."
"Who said that?" she demanded.
Toshiba put his hand up. **"Lee Iacocca, 1982!!" he said.**

Sign on a butcher's shop in London:
"We make sausages for Queen Elizabeth 11"
Sign on rival shop across the street said **"God save the Queen"**

Delayed reaction
Who says the English do not have a sense of humour? In fact, if you tell a joke to an Englishman, he will laugh three times. **Once when you tell it to him, once when you explain it to him and once in the middle of the night when he gets it!!**

Courtesy Russian style ...
An American tourist in Moscow wanted to ease himself badly. Unable to find any place, he just went down to one of the side streets to take care of business.
Before he could even unzip a Moscow police officer said, "Hey you! You can't do that here. Look, follow me."
The police officer led him to a beautiful garden with lots of grass, pretty flowers and manicured hedges.
"Here," said the cop, "whiz away."
The American turns, unzips and starts right on the flowers. "Ahhh. Whew. Thanks. This is very nice of you. Is this Russian courtesy?" asked the tourist.
"No. This is the American Embassy!!"

Sign in a Budapest zoo:
"Please do not feed the animals. If you have any suitable food, give it to the guard on duty"

His preference ...
A moron was filling up an application form for a job.
He promptly filled columns NAME, AGE, ADDRESS; but got lost on column "SEX".
After much thought, he wrote **"THRICE A WEEK"**.
He was then told it was wrong and to write MALE or FEMALE.
Again, the moron thought for a long time. Finally, he wrote **"PREFERABLY FEMALES"!!**

High finance
An Indian walks into a bank in New York City and asks for the loan officer. He says he is going to Europe on business for two weeks and needs to borrow $5,000. The bank officer says the bank will need some kind of security for such a loan, so the guy hands over the keys of a new Mercedes parked on the street in front of the bank. The bank agrees to accept the car as collateral for the loan.

Two weeks later, the man returns, repays the $5,000 and the interest, which comes to $15.41.

The loan officer says, "We're very happy to have had your business, but we are a little puzzled. While you were away, we checked your Bank a/c and found that you are a multi-millionaire. What puzzles us is why would you needed to borrow ONLY $5,000?"

The Indian replied, **"Where else in New York can I park my car for two weeks for 15 bucks!!!"**

A mystery ...
India's worst air disaster occurred today when a small two-seater plane crashed into a cemetery early this morning in central Punjab.
Sardar officials search and rescue workers have recovered 1,204 bodies so far and expect that number to climb as digging continues into the night.

It pays to be patient ...
Three guys are about to be executed and they are asked what they wish to have for their last meal.
Italian: "Pepperoni Pizza"
He is served and then executed.
Frenchman: "Filet Mignon."
He is served and then executed.
Jew: "Strawberries."
Jailor: "But they are out of season!"
Jew: "I'll wait!!!"

A bargain ...
A Young Aussie was enjoying his first night in Rome drinking cappuccino at a pavement cafe when a pretty girl came and sat beside him.
"Hello," he said. "Do you understand English?"
"Only a little," she answered.
"How much?" he asked."
"$50" she replied!!

You reap what you sow ...
The Indian chief appeared before the justice for a divorce. The Justice asked the chief for a reason. The Indian Chief answered, "When we plant corn, we get corn. When we plant spinach, we get spinach. When we plant barley, we get barley. **But me plant Indian and me get Chinaman, me want divorce."**

Not the oil but how you use it ...
Three old men are discussing their sex lives. The Italian man says, "Last week, my wife and I had great sex. I rubbed her body with olive oil, made passionate love and she screamed for five minutes at the end."
The Frenchman boasts, "Hey, I rubbed my wife's body with butter, made passionate love and she screamed for 15 minutes!"
The Jewish man says, "Well, last week we had sex too but I used chicken fat and she screamed for **6** hours."
The Italian and Frenchman were stunned. They asked, "What did you do to make her scream for **six** hours???"
"I wiped my hands on the drapes!"

It was reported in a survey that when the first Viagra Baby was born in Japan, he weighed:
6 Pounds and 12 Inches.
(Incidentally "12 Inches" refers to the height of the Baby.)

Business

You see a gorgeous girl at a party. You go up to her and say, "I'm fantastic in bed."
That's Direct Marketing

You're at a party with a bunch of friends and see a gorgeous girl. One of your friends goes up to her and pointing at you says, "He's fantastic in bed."
That's Advertising

You see a gorgeous girl at a party. You go up to her and get her telephone number. The next day you call and say, "Hi, I'm fantastic in bed."
That's Telemarketing

You're at a party and see a gorgeous girl. You get up and straighten your tie; you walk up to her and pour her a drink. You open the door for her, pick up her bag after she drops it, offer her a ride, and then say, "By the way, I'm fantastic in bed."
That's Public Relations

You're at a party and see a gorgeous girl. She walks up to you and says, "I hear you're fantastic in bed."
That's Brand Recognition

"There's a way of transferring funds that is even faster than electronic banking. It's called **marriage**."
- James Holt McGauran

A kiss is a strange thing. A small boy gets it for nothing. A young man has to steal it. And an old man has to pay for it.

❖

Boss: Someone who is early when you are late and late when you are early.

❖

A moron went to a newly opened restaurant. After his meal he was given a "feedback" form to fill.
The moron looked at the form and started removing his sweater and shirt. He was about to remove his pants when the shocked waiter said, "Sir, what are you doing?"
The moron replied, "See what it says here! **'Fill this form in brief'** ".

❖

A saleswoman from a major condom company, carrying a briefcase of various samples, went to meet a perspective buyer. As she jumped into the cab, she dropped her briefcase and all the condoms flew out all over the floor in front of all the other passengers. They all stared amazed at the display and then looked to the woman who said sheepishly, **"I'm meeting a new client."**

❖

New Definitions

Divorce: Future tense of marriage.

Cigarette: A pinch of tobacco rolled in paper with fire at one end and a fool on the other.

Conference: The confusion of one man multiplied by the number present.

Compromise: The art of dividing a cake in such a way that everybody believes he got the biggest piece.

Tears: The hydraulic force by which masculine will-power is defeated by feminine water power...

Conference Room: A place where everybody talks, nobody listens and everybody disagrees later on.

Committee: Individuals who can do nothing individually and sit to decide that nothing can be done together.

Experience: The name men give to their mistakes.

Diplomat: A person who tells you to go to hell in such a way that you actually look forward to the trip.

Father: A banker provided by nature.

Miser: A person who lives poor so that he can die rich.

❖